atlas.jc.c

'territorial evolution' — natural process
reification
(Marx).
historical maps

THROUGH THE MACKENZIE BASIN

Metonymy: contiguous relationship

dogs: natives

— Flaubert / D. H. Lawrence
— place characters next
to telling images

Charles Mair
Reprinted from Charles Mair's
Tecumseh, a drama; and, Canadian poems,
2nd ed. (Toronto: William Briggs, 1901).

Through the
MACKENZIE BASIN

An Account of the
Signing of Treaty No. 8
and the
Scrip Commission, 1899

Charles Mair

Introductions by
David W. Leonard
Brian Calliou

Western Canada Reprint Series

 The University of Alberta Press

Edmonton & District Historical Society

Published by

The University of Alberta Press and
the Edmonton & District Historical Society
Athabasca Hall
Edmonton, Alberta, Canada T6G 2E8

This edition copyright © The University of Alberta Press 1999

ISBN 0–88864–326–8
ISSN 0820–9561;6

Canadian Cataloguing in Publication Data

Mair, Charles, 1838–1927.
  Through the Mackenzie basin

  (Western Canada reprint series, ISSN 0820–9561 ; 6)
  Reprint. Originally published: Toronto : W. Briggs, 1908.
  Copublished by: Edmonton & District Historical Society.
  Includes bibliographical references and index.
  ISBN 0–888864–326–8

  1. Athabasca and Peace River Treaty Expedition (1899) 2. Northwest,
Canadian—History—1870-1905. 3. Indians of North America—Canada—
Treaties. 4. Alberta—Description and travel. I. Leonard, David, 1945- II.
Calliou, Brian. III. Historical Society of Alberta. Edmonton and District
Historical Society. IV. Title. V. Series.
FC3217.M34 1999   971.2'02   C98–911083–4
F1060.9.M34 1999

Printed on acid-free paper. ∞

Printed and bound in Canada by Priority Printing Ltd., Edmonton, Alberta.

The University of Alberta Press gratefully acknowledges the support
received for its publishing program from The Canada Council for the Arts
and the Government of Canada through the Book Publishing Industry
Development Program.

Canadä

THE CANADA COUNCIL | LE CONSEIL DES ARTS
FOR THE ARTS | DU CANADA
SINCE 1957 | DEPUIS 1957

To the memory of Charles Mair

CONTENTS

ACKNOWLEDGEMENTS

The release of this reprint in 1999 is most timely, given the growing interest in Treaty No. 8 and the concurrent distribution of scrip, as well as the 100th anniversary of the events of 1899 in the North-West Territories, of which this book is so revealing.

A special thanks to Brian Calliou for undertaking to provide his perspective on *Through the Mackenzie Basin* and on Treaty No. 8. With his personal and professional knowledge of the region, and the issues surrounding the Treaty, his views add considerably to this reprint.

I would also like to thank the directorship of the University of Alberta Press for publishing this important source for sub-arctic Canadian history, and for their confidence in me to edit and introduce this new edition. Special thanks to editor Mary Mahoney-Robson.

Thanks also to the Edmonton & District Historical Society for serving as copublisher and for their interest in the history of the regions north of Edmonton.

Additional funding for the new edition of *Through the Mackenzie Basin* has come from The Western Canadiana Publications Project as part of its Western Canada Reprint Series. The interest and efforts of Ken Munro and Rod Macleod in the Department of History and Classics at the University of Alberta, for including this in its historical reprint series is especially appreciated.

The Historic Sites Service of Alberta Community Development and its Research and Publications Program is also to be thanked for their interest in the North and for making some of my time available to undertake this work. Kathryn Ivany, John Geiger, Michael Payne, Don Wetherell and Ken Tingley all took time to review and comment on my own small contribution.

David Leonard

PREFACE

When *Through the Mackenzie Basin* was published by William Briggs in 1908, it became an immediate success as an adventure book on the unsettled regions of Northwest Canada. In later years, its main value has been to provide primary source information for the study of Treaty No. 8 and the accompanying distribution of scrip in the District of Athabaska in 1899. Mair had been a Secretary to the Half-breed Scrip Commission that year, and had kept a diary of his observations and impressions. This formed the basis of *Through the Mackenzie Basin*, with many passages being verbatim from the diary. Today, the diary is held among Mair's other papers at Queen's University Archives at Kingston, Ontario.

The title of *Through the Mackenzie Basin* is misleading, for, in fact, the author and the party in which he travelled did not go beyond Smith's Portage (Fitzgerald) in 1899. To make the work a more general northern study, Mair and his publisher decided to combine it with a large chapter on "The Mammals and Birds of Northern Canada" by the former Hudson's Bay Company trader, Roderick MacFarlane. Because MacFarlane's chapter adds nothing to our current understanding of the subject, it has been omitted from this reprint. As this is a facsimile edition, the original pagination has been kept. Mr. Côté's Poem, originally on page 490 of the original edition, immediately follows the Mair account in this edition. The complete text of Treaty No. 8, the Order In Council and the Report of the Commissioners for Treaty No. 8 have been reprinted from Canada, *Statutes*, 63 Victoria, A. 1900, Sessional Paper No. 14, instead of the unsigned text of Treaty No. 8 in the original edition.

It is not known for sure who shot the photographs used in this book. In all likelihood, camera-work was undertaken by several officers of the North-West Mounted Police who were part of the excursion of 1899. An album containing these and other western Canadian images was borrowed from Superintendent H.C. Forbes of the RCMP for copying by the Glenbow Archives in Calgary in the late 1950s, according to Hugh Dempsey. As a number of the images are blurred, slanted or out of focus, it would appear that the photographer(s) would have been amateurs. In later years, this album was presented by Parks Canada to the Saskatchewan Archives Board, Saskatoon Campus, being identified as "Major Walker's Photo Album." Walker was one of the Treaty Commissioners of 1899, and a former member of the North-West Mounted Police. The Saskatchewan Archives Board still holds this album. Prints from the album, and other photos taken of the North-West Territories in 1899 by O.C. Edwards, are held by the Glenbow Archives in fonds NA-949 and NA-4035.

Many issues addressed in *Through the Mackenzie Basin* are topical and contentious, particularly those relating to Treaty No. 8 and the scrip allotment of 1899. My Introduction and Brian Calliou's "Prelude to Expansion" are intended to place this reprint in historical perspective. We believe that this valuable primary source document will be of great assistance to all scholars engaged in the study of the history of Northwest Canada, particularly those concerned with Canada's First Nations. We hope the book will also be read by others as a lively and informative account of people, places and events in the lands north of Edmonton in 1899, albeit from the perspective of a government supporter, ardent Canadian nationalist and firm believer in the British institutions of his time.

INTRODUCTION

Charles Mair
and the Settlement of 1899

When *Through the Mackenzie Basin* was published in 1908, it marked the culmination of the literary career of one of Canada's most passionately nationalist writers, Charles Mair.[1] Then an official with the federal immigration service, Mair had accompanied the Treaty No. 8 Commission and the Half-breed Scrip Commission throughout what is now northern Alberta as one of its official secretaries during the summer of 1899. Notes compiled while on this excursion were used as the basis of his subsequent account, which is a lively and detailed description of the people, events and scenery witnessed at the time.[2] The work is presented from the perspective of a lover of the wilderness and a strong apologist for the British Empire, whose reputation and expressed world view could warrant his designation as the Rudyard Kipling of Canada.[3]

As the Treaty and the Scrip Commissions travelled only as far as Smith's Landing (Fitzgerald), the title of *Through the Mackenzie Basin* is in some ways misleading. It was the original publisher's decision to broaden the scope of the book and include a study on "The Birds and Mammals of Northern Canada" by Roderick MacFarlane. As MacFarlane's work adds nothing to our understanding of Mair's travels, it has been omitted from this reprint. Mair's purpose in compiling his account was to provide the reader with a revealing and engaging description of a part of the country with which most Canadians were largely unfamiliar. It followed upon and added to the publications of such other popular adventure writers as William Francis Butler (*The Wild North Land*, 1874), Wharburton Pike (*The Barren Grounds of Northern Canada*, 1892), and H. Somers Somerset (*Land of the Muskeg*, 1895).[4]

As a documentary source however, Mair's book was special. It was written by a first-hand witness to some of the most significant events in the history of Northwest Canada, namely the signing of Treaty No. 8 at Lesser Slave Lake, and certain other adhesions that followed. Mair was also a direct participant in the details of the initial distribution of scrip in the region that summer. In addition to the official documents, his account has come to constitute the most detailed published source for the interpretation of these events, although obviously written by a decided government apologist.

At the time of publication, the full ramifications of the Treaty signing and scrip allotment were not readily apparent, for the land in the Unorganized District of Athabaska remained largely unsettled. The Klondike gold rush had petered out, mineral resources along the lower Athabasca River had yet to be tapped, and the Peace River Country was still awaiting the settlement rush long predicted for it. Reserves had been surveyed for several of the native bands who had taken Treaty, including certain parcels in severalty.[5] A number of holdings had also been marked out for those who had preferred settlement by land scrip. Most of those who had opted for money scrip had chosen to sell their entitlement, but were living off the land anyway. In 1908, most northerners lived pretty much as they had prior to the time of the settlement, either within or outside their assigned holdings. The most pronounced change in the region was in the economy, where, by now, cash had replaced barter as the standard form of exchange.

During the next ten years, change would be more dramatic. In 1909, a Dominion Land Office was opened at Grouard. The next five years would see the first wave of agricultural settlement to the Peace River Country. In 1910, Alfred von Hammerstein formed the Athabasca Oil and Asphalt Company. That same year, the Alberta government committed itself to railway extension to Waterways near Fort McMurray as well as the Peace Country. Six years later, the Edmonton, Dunvegan and British Columbia Railway would reach Peace River and Grande Prairie, and bring further settlement to this district. At the same time, the first scientific experiments on the bituminous sands around Fort McMurray were being undertaken by Sidney Ells. When the railway reached Waterways in 1921, more comprehensive experiments on extraction were begun by Karl Clark.

These developments brought an influx of Euro-Canadian developers whose views on the exploitive possibilities of the land stood in stark contrast to those of people who subsisted with the environment. The resulting cultural disparity would bring into greater focus the terms of the Treaty and eventually call into question the inherent meaning of both the spoken and written words of the Treaty and Scrip Commissioners, as well as the perceived understanding of those who had either taken Treaty or had agreed to the offer of scrip. In this context, the words recorded by Charles Mair have had, and will continue to have much significance in the affairs of the Northwest.

Through the Mackenzie Basin contains no prognosis of any future conflict or misinterpretation of the events of 1899. Throughout the narrative, Mair's tone is decidedly one of optimism. The settlement process was seen as peaceful, with the natives basically satisfied, having resisted certain disruptive elements bent on scuttling the negotiations, described by Mair as "half-breeds…from Edmonton, who had been vitiated by contact with a low class of white man there."[6] That Mair should have presented such a picture is not surprising. He was a passionate Canadian and an advocate of the benevolence of the British Empire. His poems and other writings also reveal a strong affinity for the wilderness and an empathy for the plight of the North American Indian.

A personal friend of Treaty Commissioner David Laird, Mair had demonstrated his commitment to the cause of Canadian expansion during the Red River Rebellion of 1869–70 and the North-West Rebellion of 1885. His vision for western Canada saw the welfare of native peoples inextricably tied to the spread of Euro-Canadian and, hence, British institutions. Little wonder that the Treaty signing and scrip allotment of 1899 was depicted by Mair as fair and equitable for "a very worthy people, whose progress in the forms of civilized life, and to a certain extent its elegances, was a constant surprise to us."[7] For the most part, subsequent accounts, both published and unpublished, have not been nearly so kind to the process, and it is as primary source material, not interpretation, that the worth of Mair's book lies to the scholars of the native history of Northwest Canada.[8]

Charles Mair was born in Lanark, Upper Canada on 21 September 1838. His family was involved in the lumber trade in the largely unreclaimed Ottawa Valley. Here, the Algonquins still occupied the forests. It was from these forests that the young Mair developed his lifelong attachment to the wilderness. From his mother, he inherited a strong taste for English literature. Following grade school, he attended grammar school at Perth, and then enrolled in the Medical Arts Program at Queen's University, Kingston. For economic reasons, he left Queen's without completing his degree and returned to his father's business in the Ottawa Valley. In 1866 however, bored with lumbering, Mair sold his interest to his brother and was back at Queen's. While there, he succeeded in publishing several poems in the Montreal *Transcript* and the Kingston *Daily News*. Two of these, entitled "The Pines" and "Summer," earned him a membership in the Botanical Society of Canada.

In 1868, Mair published his first book, *Dreamland and other Poems*, which strongly reflected his passion for the wilds.[9] It also reflected his Canadian patriotism, which was growing during this era of Confederation. On a trip to Ottawa, he made the acquaintance of one Henry J. Morgan, through whom he became a member of an informal club of brash young nationalists called Canada First. Being, for the most part, well-to-do professionals and businessmen, these patriots were determined to see Canada's destiny rest on greater self-reliance and exertion of her own national will. In the cause of Canada, they were not unlike the manifest destiny advocates in the United States, whom the Canada Firsters regarded as the major threat to the future of their country.

Another individual who was having a profound effect on Mair's outlook was a physician named John Schultz, whom Mair had met at Queen's. Schultz had gone on to establish a medical practice in the Red River Settlement, and, through his letters, Mair began to develop an interest in the British Northwest. Another acquaintance at this time was William McDougall, then federal Minister of Public Works. Impressed by the young patriotic literateur and his keen interest in nature, McDougall invited Mair to serve as accountant and paymaster for a construction party on its way to Lake-of-the-Woods to push through a road for anticipated immigrants. Mair was urged to forward descriptive accounts of the region for publication in the eastern press in order to attract more settlers. What resulted was a series of letters to the Montreal *Gazette* and the Toronto *Globe* which, in their attention to detail, if not accuracy, foretold the quality of description later to appear in *Through the Mackenzie Basin*.

Mair and the construction party arrived at Fort Garry in October 1868, having travelled by way of Chicago and St. Paul. These were traumatic times in the Red River Settlement, for Canada was now negotiating the purchase of the lease on

Rupert's Land from the Hudson's Bay Company. This was causing considerable unrest among the Métis population along the Red River, for they were not being consulted as to the future of the Northwest. At the time, there were close to 10,000 Métis in the region, of both French and Scottish ancestry. This compared to about 1,500 Euro-Canadians and 500 Indians. The Métis were worried about the legal status of the land on which they lived, and apprehensive that incorporation within Canada would signal an end to their way of life. They received considerable sympathy from employees of the Hudson's Bay Company who wished to see a continuance of the fur trade as opposed to large scale farming. In opposition to the Métis was a close-knit group of Canadian expansionists, of whom Mair's friend, John Schultz, was a vocal and ubiquitous spokesman. Now a merchant in Winnipeg, Schultz and his exploitive ways had succeeded in alienating a large number of Métis in and around the Settlement.

With his ties to Canada First and his attachment to Schultz, Mair also drew the hostility of many Métis. Symbolising his expansionist views was the road construction project in which he was engaged, which was obviously intended to facilitate settlers from the East. Resentment grew when payment for road work turned out to be in the form of credit to Schultz's store, where goods were over-priced. Furthermore, Mair's dispatches to the eastern press, which were drifting back to the Settlement, did not mention the hard times endured by the Métis, but instead portrayed conditions as idyllic for prospective settlers. As his overall unpopularity grew, Mair confined his social activities increasingly to the small, but dedicated group of Canadian expansionists. One of these was Elizabeth McKenny, the twenty-year-old niece of John Schultz, whom Mair married in September 1869.

During that fall, tension mounted along the Red River. The sale of Rupert's Land had been completed and a newly-appointed Lieutenant-Governor for the North-West Territories, William

McDougall, was scheduled to institute the reins of government on 1 December 1869. Even prior to then, government surveyors began to mark out quarter sections in anticipation of a rush of settlers from the East. This was in contrast to the river lot system of plots that had previously been adopted from Quebec. On 16 October, a National Committee of the Métis of Red River was formed. At the time, Mair was on his honeymoon in Minnesota, but decided to return to the Settlement in the company of Lieutenant-Governor McDougall, who was then on his way to Fort Garry. On their way northward, the party encountered Joseph Howe who had been dispatched to the Settlement to investigate the unrest and report back to Prime Minister John A. Macdonald. Howe warned McDougall not to take rash action. Shortly thereafter, he warned McDougall by letter to avoid dealing with the group of expansionist hotheads led by John Schultz. As McDougall's party continued northward, they received another note, this being from Louis Riel, who instructed McDougall not to enter the Red River Settlement.

Blistering from what they perceived to be an affront to Canada, Mair and his wife proceeded to Winnipeg, leaving McDougall and his party at Pembina to await further instructions from Ottawa. Shortly after crossing the border, the Mairs were arrested by a contingent of Métis. Elizabeth was taken to a convent at St. Norbert and Charles to the home of the resident priest. A few days later, Riel led a band of over 100 Métis followers into Fort Garry and assumed command of the post. His declared purpose was to secure a consultative voice for his people in the destiny of the Canadian Northwest.

On 4 November, Mair and his wife were released from custody on the promise that they would leave the Red River Settlement. True to his impulsive nature, Mair agreed, but instead headed straight for Schultz's store in Winnipeg, where plans were being formulated to take back Fort Garry. While Riel and his Committee drew up a Bill of Rights to present to the federal government, McDougall and his party crossed the border on 1 December and issued a proclamation claiming the North-West Territories for Canada. They then returned to the safety of Pembina. In the meantime, Schultz, Mair and 46 other Canadian patriots began to fortify Schultz's store and adjacent buildings and await the arrival of federal forces. In response, Riel placed two loaded cannon in front of the store and demanded the surrender of the occupants. Facing possible death, the defiant expansionists surrendered and were confined as prisoners in Fort Garry. Here, they were treated liberally. Mair, however, was confronted by Riel for having lied by remaining in the Settlement. Mair replied by declaring Riel a traitor who was now standing in the way of Canada's destiny.[10]

On 9 January 1870, Mair and six other prisoners managed to escape. Mair headed for the cottage of a known sympathiser and was soon on his way to Portage La Prairie where the cause of Canada had a larger following. With Schultz, who had also escaped, and one Thomas Scott, Mair began to solicit support and plan an attack on Fort Garry. Fanning the flames was an incident in which a Métis youth shot and killed a young Scots farmer, whereupon the Métis was beaten to death. Shortly thereafter, rumours circulated that Riel intended to capture and execute the leaders of the expansionist resistance. Mair and a small party thus departed for St. Paul, arriving there on 23 March after a harsh journey. Here, he learned of the execution of Thomas Scott by Riel's provisional government, and also of the decision of Prime Minister Macdonald to defer the establishment of a government in the North-West Territories until the case for the Red River Métis could be fully heard and considered. Professing shock at these developments, Mair soon set out for Toronto to take the cause of the expansionists straight to the people of Ontario. He was accompanied by Schultz, who had also eluded capture, and several other supporters.

In Toronto, Mair, Schultz and their party were greeted by a swell of support nurtured by their Canada First friends. In addressing a rally, Mair gushed forth a volley of rhetoric that demonstrated without question his opinion of certain ethnic cultures:

> Why should the most bigoted portions of the inhabitants be able to overcome those possessed of property and intellect? The French at Red River delight in having all the whiskey they can drink and as little to do as they could possibly have. The capture of the loyal settlers was the result of treachery on the part of the Hudson's Bay Company and the Roman Catholic clergy. The death of our brother, Thomas Scott, at the hands of the barbarians shall not be unavenged.[11]

Mair and Schultz then proceeded to Ottawa, addressing crowds along the way. Ironically, Louis Riel was also in Ottawa with a delegation, declaring for the rights of the Métis. Feeling his hands tied, Macdonald at first did nothing. Eventually, however, he dispatched a detachment to the Settlement under Colonel Garnet Wolseley, ostensibly to maintain order. When Wolseley arrived, his purpose to put down any further attempt at rebellion became obvious to all. As Riel fled across the border into the United States, Wolseley took charge of Fort Garry. On 12 May 1870, the province of Manitoba was formed. Though certain gains had been achieved by the Métis, many of them now began to move further westward, leaving much land open for settlement by Euro-Canadians.

With the Red River Rebellion over, Mair and his wife settled at Portage La Prairie and opened a general store. Mair also invested in land and placed ads in eastern newspapers encouraging prospective settlers to move to the area. By 1877, he and Elizabeth had five children and had gained some wealth. Mair appeared to be restless with the growing settlement however, and, in 1878, he and his family moved to Prince Albert, where prospects for future development appeared bright.

The Canadian Pacific Railway seemed certain to pass through the district. Mair again opened a store and again undertook to speculate in land. Here, his perspective of Métis culture began to change somewhat, and, on more than one occasion, he found himself declaring his support for the plight of the plains Métis, particularly in light of the rapidly disappearing buffalo.

During the early 1880s, the same apprehension about Canadian expansion that had gripped the Métis of Red River became rife along the Saskatchewan Rivers. The Canadian Pacific Railway, which entered the region in 1882, appeared to symbolise future dominance by Euro-Canadian settlers. With tensions mounting, and many Métis calling for the return of Louis Riel, Mair decided to send his family back east, to a home recently purchased in Windsor. In 1883, with Riel now back in western Canada, Mair decided to join his family in Windsor until the troubles blew over. His growing sympathy for the Métis had not extended to support for rebellion, and certainly not to forgiveness of Riel. Nor could Mair remain passive in the coming conflict, and, with the outbreak of hostilities, he volunteered his services as a telegrapher at Humboldt in the District of Saskatchewan. When the North-West Rebellion was over, Mair applauded the execution of Riel.

While in Windsor, Mair composed his most noteworthy and popular literary work, a play on the life of Tecumseh.[12] It was dedicated to "The Survivors of the Canada First Association." Significantly, the main character emerges not so much as a charismatic defender of his people as a forward thinking leader, wisely preferring British civilization to that of the Americans. Despite the wide acclaim that Tecumseh received in the East, Mair had nonetheless come to stake his own identity on the West, and, so, in 1886, he moved his family back to Prince Albert. Here he resumed life as a merchant and also found time to continue writing. Poems such as "The Last Buffalo" reveal his concern for the native and the natural environment of the West. His advocacy helped move the federal government to create a buffalo reserve near present day Wainwright, and brought for Mair election to the Royal Society of Canada.

Prosperity, however, did not continue in Prince Albert. The CPR had missed the community, intersecting Regina instead, and land values had tumbled. With high CPR freight rates, merchandizing in the region was also in decline. During the early 1890s, Mair began to seek opportunities elsewhere. He even travelled to the United States in an attempt to lure former Canadians back to Canada, to settle in the West. In 1892, he began a short-lived real estate office in St. Paul, proclaiming the richness of Canada's "last best west." He also set up an exhibit at the Chicago World's Fair the following year, pronouncing the same message, but with few results.

Upon returning to Prince Albert, Mair was successful in convincing a banker to back a fur trading operation on the Mackenzie River. He was about to undertake this venture when a persuasive letter from his daughter and son-in-law in the Okanagan Valley convinced him that he should recommence general merchandizing with a store somewhere in the Valley. Leaving Elizabeth to work in Prince Albert as a postmistress, Mair travelled west and succeeded in establishing a general store at Okanagan Mission, and, shortly thereafter, in Kelowna. Here he was soon joined by Elizabeth. Success was fleeting however, and, in 1894, Elizabeth returned to Prince Albert to resume her postal duties and keep up the Prince Albert property. Two years later, when his store folded in Kelowna, Mair went back to Prince Albert.

Now almost 60 years of age and somewhat dispirited, Mair undertook odd jobs in Prince Albert until he was offered a position with the Department of the Interior in Winnipeg. No doubt, one of his earlier government acquaintances had heard of his plight and taken pity. This was possibly the former Minister of the Interior, David Laird, whom Mair had earlier befriended in Prince Albert.[13] The job was with the Western Immigration Service, with which Mair had some experience.

The new Interior Minister, Clifford Sifton, had embarked on a new course for immigration that would seek settlers from eastern as well as western Europe. In 1898, Mair was instrumental in assisting a colony of Doukhobors settle in the Swan River district of northern Saskatchewan. For the next 23 years, and well into retirement, he would work with the Immigration Service in locating homes for settlers, and engage in other Departmental projects. All the while, he continued to compose poetry and undertake other literary and journalistic ventures.

It was Mair's extensive experience with the Métis and land settlement in the West that brought Clifford Sifton to seek his services for the Half-breed Scrip Commission in 1899. This was probably through the advice of David Laird, who had been appointed Treaty Commissioner. With his literary talents, it was understandable that Mair be appointed one of the Commission's Secretaries, the other being J.F. Prudhomme of St. Boniface. Mair thus travelled to Edmonton in May 1899, and, here, his narrative would begin. On 29 May 1899, the Treaty and Scrip Commissions left Edmonton in a contingent of about 50 people and headed north to Athabasca Landing, then west to Lesser Slave Lake, where, at the west end, the largest concentration of native people in the Athabaska Territory was gathering. At a spot off the Lake, which would later form part of Grouard, the initial negotiations for Treaty No. 8 commenced on 20 June. The next day, six Cree spokesmen, described by the Treaty Commissioners, and Mair, as "chiefs," inscribed their "X" on the Treaty document earlier drawn up by the Commissioners.[14] The following day, the onerous business of scrip allotment began with those resident natives who had not taken treaty.[15]

The events at Lesser Slave Lake during 20 and 21 June effectively concluded the bargaining phase of Treaty No. 8. Henceforth, all other northern bands or Indian families would be required to either adhere to the terms established at the Lakehead or remain non-treaty Indians. At most spots visited, adhesions were secured, although many people were missed due to lingering hesitancy or because the Commissioners were over two weeks behind schedule. When their work was concluded in September, and both the Scrip and Treaty Commissions back in Edmonton, the government was still not certain whether or not they had dealt with the majority of the natives within the Treaty boundary, which had been arbitrarily set by Laird.[16] Thus, in the summer of 1900, another Commission, led by J.A. McRae, traversed the same region, following, again and again, the same procedures. With the Treaty adhesions and scrip allotments of 1900, the government felt safe in concluding that the majority of native peoples within the Treaty boundaries had accepted an extinguishment to any claim on the land outside their scrip or reserve entitlements.

The decision to initiate settlement had not come easily in the first place. Unlike most natives to the South, the northern peoples did not live in tribal social structures, seldom recognized chiefs who could speak without question on their behalf, and were scattered throughout countless communities and camps, many impossible to locate, let alone travel to. Furthermore, so much intermixing of people had taken place that it was often impossible to identify what band a family was traditionally a part of, or whether or not an individual had traces of European ancestry. Also, the Northwest held many people who had been settled with earlier, either with Treaty No. 6 in 1876, or the 1885 allotment of scrip. Names frequently changed with time or took alternate spellings. Deciding eligibility for all claimants became a challenging task, and never would be fully resolved.

Nonetheless, during the late 1890s, the North-West Territories had appeared to be on the verge of large scale settlement. The rich soil in the Peace River Country had long been touted, while the Klondike gold rush was drawing the attention of the entire continent to the mineral resources in the Yukon. The Klondike rush was also making evident what disruption uncontrolled exploitation could cause in northern communities. Thus, in the spring of 1898, it was decided to initiate a settlement. Its dual purpose was to secure an extinguishment of the natives' claim to the land, and to provide the Unorganized District of Athabaska, as well as certain lands beyond, with a foundation for Euro-Canadian law, social order, culture, and economic development.

At the time of the decision, prognosis was that the Indians of the Northwest were not then anxious for a treaty.[17] During the next year therefore, missionaries and North-West Mounted Police were urged to convey to these people the perspective that settlement would be in their best interest. The missionaries and police complied. On the eve of the initial signing however, it was still not certain whether a majority of the Indians would be agreeable. For this reason, Treaty Commissioner James Ross travelled to Lesser Slave Lake ahead of the two Commissions to alleviate fears. To the Treaty Commission itself was added the most highly respected priest in the North-West Territories, Father Albert Lacombe. At Lesser Slave Lake, Lacombe was joined by Bishop Emile Grouard. Present for the Anglicans were Reverends George Holmes and W.G. White.

There was much drama played out at Lesser Slave Lake in the days leading up to the Treaty signing. No one seemed to know for sure how the locals would respond to the Commissioners' overtures. The Cree of the district appeared to be genuinely concerned that treaty would confine them to reserves and that game laws would restrict their hunting and fishing. There was also a rumour afloat that accepting treaty would subject the natives to the British Army draft for service in the Boer War.[18] A delegation from Whitefish (now Utikima) Lake did not show up for the negotiations, while, from Sturgeon Lake, only 22 people were present.

For the government, success at Lesser Slave Lake was critical to prospects of settlement elsewhere, for news of success or failure would surely reverberate throughout the Northwest. Tactically, the Commissioners decided to undertake treaty negotiations before scrip allotment, for those natives opting for scrip would certainly be favourable to a settlement as they had nothing to lose. They would consequently provide pressure for the others to accept treaty. Conceptually, treaty had been intended only for the Indians of the region, and scrip for the Métis. However, it was decided to offer scrip in place of treaty to any northern resident with elements of indigenous ancestry, for so many did not know whether or not they had any traces of European blood. On the eve of settlement, it was estimated that about two-thirds of the people at Lesser Slave Lake would opt for scrip.[19]

The missionaries, police and most government officials had advised the Indians to take treaty. This would provide 160 acres of reserve land per individual, taken either in proximity to other families or apart as severalty. Treaty was also to ensure equipment and supplies for farming, training and schooling for the children, a $12 settlement bonus, and an annuity of $5 per person in perpetuity. On the other hand, those opting for scrip would be issued a certificate entitling them to either a tract of 240 acres of land or an evaluation of $240 that could be used towards the eventual purchase of Crown land anywhere. Other people who had settled in the region and had made improvements to their holdings would be granted these holdings outright to the extent of 160 acres apiece.

To ensure that everyone would be settled with land as opposed to cash, the government had initially determined that the scrip notes should not be made transferable, or allowed to be signed over to someone else. However, to many northern natives, the transfer provision was what gave value to the scrip. They reasoned that they could settle on northern lands anyway, and, therefore, the real estate provided by the scrip had little meaning to them. However, to individuals dealing with land in the southern regions, these valuations could have significant worth, and many present at the signing proved to be only too glad to purchase the scrip notes for use elsewhere, usually at less than half of their face value. Not wishing to jeopardize the signing, the Commissioners gave way to pressure and agreed to alter their provision on the eve of the settlement, and the scrip notes were then altered and made transferable. The decision was made by David Laird, but was concurred with by Clifford Sifton and apologized for in the House of Commons by the Member representing the region, Frank Oliver, who said:

> In regard to the scrip buyers who follow the commission, let it be understood that these men and the money which they pay for the scrip, that alone makes it valuable in the eye of the half-breed. If the half-breed cannot turn the scrip into money, he does not want the scrip. Anyway, why should he? He would not consider that his title was extinguished unless he received in return something he could use.[20]

In Mair's analysis:

> …in spite of advice to the contrary urged upon them in the strongest manner by Father Lacombe, they agreed upon "the bird in the hand"—viz., upon cash scrip or nothing. This could be readily turned into money, for in the train of traders, etc., who followed up the treaty payments, there were also buyers from Winnipeg and Edmonton, well supplied with cash, to purchase all the scrip that offered, at great reduction, of course, from face value. Whether the half-breeds were wise or foolish is needless to say. One thing was plain, they had made up their minds.[21]

The issue of transferable scrip would prove to be the most contentious one of all during the negotiations of 1899.

It was in his account of the events at Lesser Slave Lake that Mair contributed most to the later understanding of the Treaty signing and scrip allotment, although, as has been pointed out, he provided "maddeningly little" information about the details of the work done.[22] Mair's narrative rather concentrates on describing circumstances, the environment and the people present, native or visitor. Indeed, there were many individuals on hand who had played or would play a prominent role in the development of the Northwest. Not only had David Laird been Minister of the Interior, he had also served as Lieutenant-Governor of the North-West Territories, and had negotiated Treaty No. 7 with the Blackfoot Confederacy in 1877. Father Lacombe and Bishop Grouard were two of the most highly regarded members of the Missionary Oblates of Mary Immaculate. George Holmes and W.G. White were also highly respected as Anglican missionaries. James Cornwall and Fletcher Bredin would go on to become a powerful economic force in the Northwest in the years that followed. Richard Secord was already one of the richest men in Edmonton, whose wealth would only increase with his subsequent northern land deals. Other Edmonton businessmen included Norris & Carey, LaRue & Picard, banker G.F.R. Kirkpatrick, and the town's first mayor, Matt McCaulay. Also among the scrip-buyers was Charles Alloway from Winnipeg.

Others at the Treaty signing included Harrison Young, who had served the Hudson's Bay Company for years, as had Henry Round and Albert Tate. The fur trader, Twelve-Foot Davis, was probably the most recognizable individual in the Peace River Country, while Allie Brick would become the first Member of the Alberta Provincial Parliament to represent the riding of Peace River. Peter Gunn, for whom the community of Gunn would be named, was another well known northern trader; he would go on to represent the riding of Lac Ste. Anne from 1909 to 1917.

Inspector A.E. Snyder of the North-West Mounted Police was already well known for his excursions to the North-West Territories, while Christopher West was then recognized as a prominent physician. The Métis Sam Cunningham, who then resided at Lesser Slave Lake, had represented St. Albert in the

North-West Territorial Assembly. Other prominent locals included Keenooshayo, who would be the first "Chief" to sign the Treaty, and his brother, Moostoos, of the Sucker Creek Band. Then, of course, there was Mair himself, whose role in western Canadian history has been described.

It is in the recorded words of the Chiefs and the Commissioners that *Through the Mackenzie Basin* has most intrigued posterity. For example, the fact that Keenooshayo had not made up his mind, even at the commencement of the negotiations, is obvious when he says, in Mair's dictation of words translated by Albert Tate:

> Up to the present I have earned my own living and worked in my own way for the Queen. It is good. The Indian loves his way of living and his free life. When I understand you thoroughly I will know better what I shall do. Up to the present I have never seen the time when I could not work for the Queen, and also make my own living. I will consider carefully what you have said.[23]

That Keenooshayo was not overly impressed with the government's offer and felt culturally distinct from the Euro-Canadian Commissioners is also evident:

> You say we are brothers. I cannot understand how we are so. I live differently from you. I can only understand that Indians will benefit from a very small degree from your offer.[24]

The sense of resignation on the part of The Captain from Sturgeon Lake is also evident when we read:

> I am old now. It is indirectly through the Queen that we have lived. She has supplied in a manner

the sale shops through which we have lived. Others may think I am foolish for speaking as I do now. Let them speak as they like. I accept. When I was young I was an able man and made my living independently. But I am old and feeble and not able to do much.[25]

Even a tone of humour entered the negotiations, when Moostoos addressed Commissioner Laird:

You have called us brothers. Truly I am the younger, you the elder brother. Being the younger, if the younger ask the elder for something, he will grant his request the same as our mother the Queen.[26]

The paternalism that permeates Mair's own text was evident in Laird's opening address as well:

Red Brothers! we have come here today, sent by the Great Mother to treat with you, and this is the paper she has given to us.... As white people are coming into your country, we have thought it well to tell you what is required of you. The Queen wants all the whites, half-breeds and Indians to be at peace with one another, and to shake hands when they meet. The Queen's laws must be obeyed all over the country, both by the whites and the Indians.[27]

Of the government's terms, Mair maintained that:

...when placed before them in Mr. Laird's customary kind and lucid manner, they would be accepted by both Indians and half-breeds as the best obtainable, and as conducting in all respects to their truest and most permanent interests.[28]

To avoid appearing heavy handed, Laird declared:

> The treaty is a free offer; take it or not, just as you please. If you refuse it, there is no harm done; we will not be bad friends on that account.[29]

To Laird, however, the bottom line was that:

> The Queen owns the country, but is willing to acknowledge the Indians' claims, and offers them terms as an off-set to all of them.[30]

In short, the country was going to be opened for development anyway, therefore it would be in the best interests of the natives to accept whatever terms they could get. Also:

> One thing Indians must understand, that if they do not make a treaty they must obey the law of the land—that they will be just the same whether you make a treaty or not; the laws must be obeyed.[31]

The traditional assurance of government compliance with the Treaty in perpetuity was voiced by Father Lacombe:

> Your forest and river life will not be changed by the Treaty, and you will have your annuities, as well, year by year, as long as the sun shines and the earth remains.[32]

The paternalistic tone in the negotiations was noted by Reverend W.G. White, who confided to Bishop Richard Young that the Commissioners had looked down on the northern natives as "a set of stupids."[33] In later testimony, James Cornwall would recall that "the Commissioners had unfavourably impressed the Indians, due to their lack of knowledge of the bush Indians mode of life."[34] The Indians, however, were sufficiently favourable to agree to the Treaty in principle, for, according to Mair, once Father Lacombe had made his speech, Keenooshayo asked all those who consented to stand up. According to the Edmonton *Bulletin*, another Chief named Felix Giroux then "threatened to club anyone who would not stand up."[35] The throng of Cree then, reportedly, all stood up.[36]

As reported by Mair, uncertainty continued the following day, for the terms of the Treaty had not yet been read to the Indians. When this was done at around 2:00 PM:

> Chief Keenooshayo rose and made a speech, followed by Moostoos, both assenting to the terms, when, suddenly, and to the surprise of all, the chief, who had again begun to address the Indians, perceiving gestures of dissent from his people, suddenly stopped and sat down.[37]

More assurances were then provided, after which those Indians present evidently agreed to the settlement. Their method of consent, however, is not mentioned by Mair. In a letter to Hudson's Bay Company Commissioner W.G. Wrigley, Henry Round maintained that the final set of assurances "resulted in a general shout of approval."[38] By the authority of that "general shout," the first six "X"s were inscribed on the document to be known as Treaty No. 8. Signing for the Cree at Lesser Slave Lake were Keenooshayo, Moostoos, Charles Neesuetasis, Felix Giroux, Whapahayo and The Captain. This was done at about 6:00 PM.

Following the signing, the laborious business of scrip allotment was begun. As the Treaty Commission was well behind schedule, it was split into two, with one party under James Ross heading straight for Dunvegan and Fort St. John, and the other, with David Laird, proceeding on to Peace River Crossing and further north after Laird witnessed the initial stages of the Scrip Commission's proceedings. Laird would secure adhesions at Peace River Crossing, Fort Vermilion and Fond du Lac. Commissioners Ross and McKenna would take them at Little Red River, Fort Chipewyan, Smith's Landing, Fort McMurray, and Wabasca. With their departure from Lesser Slave Lake, festivities were in the air, and were well documented by Mair:

> It was indeed a gala time for the happy-go-lucky Lakers, and the effects of the issue and sale of scrip certificates were soon manifest in our neighbour-hood. The traders' booths were thronged with purchasers, also the refreshment tents where cigars and ginger ale were sold; and, in teepees improvised from aspen saplings, the sporting element passed the night at some interesting but easy way of losing money, illuminating their game with guttering candles, minus candle sticks, and presenting a picture worthy of an impressionist's pencil.[39]

Mair proceeded to describe the people and the environment around the Lake, as well as those of other locations along the route of the Scrip Commission, which, for the most part, followed that of the Treaty Commissioners. Unfortunately, few details about the Treaty adhesion or scrip allotment process were included in his notes. People, places and circumstances, however, received lively description.[40] Peace River Crossing and Dunvegan were the next appointments, followed by Fort Vermilion, Fort Chipewyan, Fond du Lac, Fort McMurray, Wabasca and Athabasca Landing. On 23 September, both Commissions were back in Edmonton, having travelled nearly 3,200 km.

Following the journey, Mair headed back to Winnipeg to resume work with the Immigration Service. In 1903, he was transferred to Lethbridge to deal with the growing number of

Americans coming into the West. The considerable popularity of *Through the Mackenzie Basin* after its release in 1908 came as a pleasant surprise and some solace to him, following, as it did, the death of his wife and youngest daughter, Bessie, a short while earlier. After this, Mair moved to Fort Steele, British Columbia, where he continued his work with the Immigration Service. In 1921, he finally retired at age 83 and moved to Calgary, and from there to a nursing home in Victoria, British Columbia, where he died on 27 July 1927.

Today, Mair is remembered chiefly for his poems about the wilderness and for his aggressive stand against the forces of Louis Riel during the Red River Rebellion of 1869–70. As an author however, his most important contribution to western Canada will always be the primary source information he left between the covers of *Through the Mackenzie Basin*.

David W. Leonard
Project Historian for Northern Alberta
Alberta Historic Sites Service

Notes

1. Charles Mair, *Through the Mackenzie Basin* (Toronto: William Briggs, 1908).
2. Mair's papers, including his diaries of the 1899 excursion, are held by Queen's University Archives in Kingston, Ontario.
3. The best account of Mair's life and influence is in Norman Shrive, *Charles Mair, Literary Nationalist* (Toronto: University of Toronto Press, 1965). A shorter account is Bruce McDougall, *Charles Mair* (Don Mills, Ontario: Fitzhenry & Whiteside, 1978). Mair also published 27 pages of "Memoirs and Reminiscences" which are contained in a compendium of his works entitled *Tecumseh, a Drama; and Canadian Poems* (Toronto: The Radisson Society of Canada, 1926).
4. William Francis Butler, *The Wild North Land* (London: Burns & Oates, 1915). Wharburton Pike, *The Barren Grounds of Northern Canada* (New York: MacMillan & Co., 1892). H. Somers Somerset, *The Land of the Muskeg* (London: W. Heineman, 1895).
5. "Severalty" was Treaty land located away from a general body of reserve land at the wish of a family or group who chose to live apart from other members of their band. For natives of the Northwest, who did not live in tribal social structures, this was not uncommon.
6. Mair, *Through the Mackenzie Basin*, p. 22.
7. Mair, *Through the Mackenzie Basin*, p. 91.
8. The most widely read account of all the treaties of the Canadian North-West is Rene Fumoleau, *As Long As This Land Shall Last* (Toronto: McClelland & Stewart, 1973). See also Richard Price, ed., *The Spirit of the Alberta Indian Treaties* (Montreal: Institute for the Research of Public Policy, 1987). [Reissued by the University of Alberta Press in 1987 (under its Pica Pica Press imprint) and again in 1999.]
9. See Charles Mair, *Dreamland and other Poems* (Montreal: Dawson Brothers, 1886).
10. See Shrive, pp. 97–98.
11. The Toronto *Globe*, 7 April 1870.
12. See Charles Mair, *Tecumseh, A Drama* (Toronto: Hunter, Rose, 1886).
13. For an account of Mair's relationship with Laird, see John Chalmers, *Laird of the West* (Calgary: Detselig Enterprises Ltd., 1981).
14. For an analysis of the Treaty, see the articles in Price, ed., *Spirit of Alberta Indian Treaties*. Interestingly, the original treaty document is in type. Possibly this was done at Lesser Slave Lake, but, if done in Ottawa, it meant that the Treaty was accepted entirely as presented without any alternations, and that no alternation had been anticipated.

15. For an analysis of the issue of scrip, see Joe Sawchuck, Patricia Sawchuck and Theresa Ferguson, *Metis Land Rights in Alberta, a Political History* (Edmonton: Metis Association of Alberta, 1981). See also David Hall, "The Half-breed Claims Commission," *Alberta History* 25, no. 2 (Spring 1977): 1–8.

16. See David Leonard, *Delayed Frontier: The Peace River Country to 1909* (Calgary: Detselig Enterprises Ltd., 1995), p. 33.

17. See Leonard, p. 18.

18. See Leonard, pp. 20 & 28.

19. Leonard, p. 26.

20. Canada, House of Commons, 4th Session, 8th Parliament, 14 July 1899 (*Hansard*), Vol III, p. 7521. See Sawchuck et al., pp. 140ff; Hall, pp. 5–8; and Leonard, pp. 86ff.

21. Mair, *Through the Mackenzie Basin*, p. 68.

22. See Hall, p. 6.

23. Mair, *Through the Mackenzie Basin*, p. 60. The name "Keenooshayo," meaning Fish, has had several spellings, and is the basis of the name of the community of Kinuso.

24. Mair, *Through the Mackenzie Basin*, p. 59.

25. Mair, *Through the Mackenzie Basin*, p. 61.

26. Mair, *Through the Mackenzie Basin*, p. 60.

27. Mair, *Through the Mackenzie Basin*, p. 56.

28. Mair, *Through the Mackenzie Basin*, p. 53.

29. Mair, *Through the Mackenzie Basin*, p. 56.

30. Mair, *Through the Mackenzie Basin*, p. 59.

31. Mair, *Through the Mackenzie Basin*, pp. 56–57.

32. Mair, *Through the Mackenzie Basin*, p. 63.

33. Provincial Archives of Alberta, ACA (Anglican Diocese of Athabasca) 283/23, White to Bishop Richard Young, 21 August 1899.

34. Ibid., 75.75 (Ewing Commission Exhibits), 1934.

35. The Edmonton *Bulletin*, 8 July 1899. Mair, *Through the Mackenzie Basin*, p. 63.

36. Mair, *Through the Mackenzie Basin*, p. 63.

37. Mair, *Through the Mackenzie Basin*, p. 64.

38. Hudson's Bay Company Archives, B.22/c.224, Round to Wrigley, 16 July 1899.

39. Mair, *Through the Mackenzie Basin*, p. 74.

40. The names of some individuals are disclosed in Mair's diary, but not his book. On the "Voyageurs Boat—1st line," the Steersman was Joseph Vavoyard and the Bowman Edward Brazeau. On the line were Archibald Rowland, John Rowland, Archibald Becket, Arthur Murphy Baptiste Vawer [*Voyer?*], Ilzear Brimeau and John Vayoyard. On "Mr. Cyr's Scow—2 line," the "Native Tripmen" included Pierre Cyr

as Steersman and Roger Lepesang as Bowman. The line included Izear Oger [*Auger?*], Lambert Courtoreille, Edward Durocher, Baptiste Courtoreille, Akonasse Courtoreille, St. Paul Gladue and Whitebear [*Ambrose Grey of Peace River, father-in-law of Allie Brick*]. The "Cook for 3 crews" was Christie Gibson, while LeFrance was the "Cook for Staff." The "Cook for Police" was not named. All spellings are Mair's.

PRELUDE TO EXPANSION

The Treaty 8 Commissions

...and the time will come when the ring of the Canadian axe will be heard throughout these forests, and when multitudes of comfortable homes will be hewn out of what are the almost inaccessible wilderness of to-day (Mair, *Through the Mackenzie Basin*, p. 80).

Keenooshayo has said that he cannot see how it will benefit you to take treaty. As all the rights you now have will not be interfered with, therefore anything you get in addition must be a clear gain (Commissioner Ross as quoted in Mair, *Through the Mackenzie Basin*, p. 61).

Every story has three sides, yours, mine, and the facts (Fumoleau, *As Long As This Land Shall Last*, p. 17).

As a member of a Treaty 8 First Nation, and as a person interested in Treaty 8 legal history, I was pleased to hear that Charles Mair's *Through the Mackenzie Basin* would be reprinted. Its re-release coincides with the commemoration of the centennial anniversary of the signing of Treaty No. 8 and the issuance of Métis scrip. Treaty No. 8 sets out the relationship between First Nations of the territory and the Canadian state. First Nations generally declare that this relationship with the Crown of Canada is "nation to nation."

By treating with the First Nations and issuing scrip to the Métis, the Dominion of Canada dealt with the outstanding rights of the Aboriginal peoples of the Treaty 8 area. However, the Treaty Commissioners overlooked various First Nations that were more "isolated" and this has resulted in present day land claims of which the Lubicon Lake claim is the most widely known.[1]

The signing of Treaty No. 8 was a significant historical event for Canada since a vast area of land rich with resources was "released" by the First Nations to the Dominion government in return for specified terms and other promises. Indeed, Mair describes the ceded area as "an empire in itself" and as "the most valuable portions of the Northern Anticlinal."[2] Mair describes the significance of Treaty No. 8 as "this primordial and greatest treaty of all."[3] The Treaty 8 region is vast and has brought great economic benefits such as agriculture, oil sands, forest products, and oil and gas to Canadian government and industry. However, as one Treaty 8 First Nations member has remarked, "Since the signing of Treaty 8, we've been the least to benefit from our lands—government and industry has benefitted the most."[4]

The reprint of Mair's book is significant for many reasons. First, it should help to educate Canadians about discussions at the treaty negotiations beyond what was captured in the Treaty No. 8 text. It is important for the greater Canadian population to learn more about the legal and historical relationship they have with Canada's First Peoples. They will be in a better position to understand the demands and claims made by First Nations. Mair's book can provide important extrinsic evidence of what was discussed at the Treaty 8 negotiations. The text of Treaty No. 8 did not capture the entire negotiations and promises made by the Crown representatives. Extrinsic evidence must be referred to in order to get a more complete understanding of what occurred at the Treaty 8 negotiations. Mair's book is written from his diary notes taken during his trip with the Commissioners. Thus, this reprint is an important primary source of history for Treaty 8.

Second, Mair vividly describes the actors present during the negotiations. He relates what was discussed by each person, and the role they played. One gets a sense of the dynamics at play during this historic event.

Finally, this reprint has the potential to reach a much wider audience, especially with the growth of interest in Aboriginal issues. The original issue of Mair's book is quite rare and not widely available.

To illustrate the utility of Mair's book, many historians who have studied Treaty 8, or the development of Canada's Northwest, such as Rene Fumoleau,[5] Richard Daniel,[6] Dennis Madill,[7] Bennet McCardle,[8] Richard Price,[9] John Chalmers,[10] and David Leonard,[11] among others, have relied on Mair's book for primary documentation. His book has been described as "the most detailed published account" of the treaty and scrip in the Treaty 8 territory.[12] However, Mair's account of the discussions of the treaty negotiations are no doubt an "abridged transcript."[13] The literary critic, John Garvin, commented that Mair's *Through the Mackenzie Basin* was "the work of a keen observer with exceptional knowledge of the North-West, and with rare ability in descriptive prose writing."[14] Garvin also stated that the book's "effect on migration to the Athabasca and Peace River districts was almost immediate."[15]

Besides its utility as a source for historians, this reprint can also be useful for research into treaty rights issues such as First

Nations hunting and fishing rights litigation. Research on specific claims has also benefitted from Mair's account of the discussions surrounding the Treaty 8 negotiations. Courts, at one time, followed the contract law interpretation principle of looking only at the wording of the treaties and refused to consider any extrinsic evidence. For example, in a treaty hunting case in which two elders who were present at the treaty signing were to be called as witnesses, the Alberta Magistrate remarked, "I am not going to be party to allowing a conversation of what they understood. The treaty speaks for itself."[16] However, case law has developed whereby "the courts have started to rely on the content of treaty negotiations."[17] The previous example illustrates how some judges have interpreted and understood the treaty. But this leads to the important question, what is the First Nations' understanding of Treaty 8? Their perspective of the treaty generally differs from Crown representatives in present relationships. First Nations of the Treaty 8 territory have their own source of knowledge on the treaty—oral traditions passed down through the generations. Through the knowledge of the elders, Treaty 8 First Nations view the treaty as sacred, whereby solemn promises were made to share the land and resources in a peaceful manner.[18]

As well, the treaties were written in a specific language by a government that used specific legal terminology to reflect their long history of land ownership, while the First Nations had a very different language, culture and view of the land. It is not entirely clear that there was a "meeting of the minds." Indeed, one Chief of a Treaty 8 First Nation in northeastern British Columbia stated, "the words in the treaty which say the land was 'surrendered, yielded up,' etc. when translated would mean 'I quit the land'. There is no way the Indians understood this."[19] This point needs to be more clearly understood by Canadians. The different interpretations of Treaty No. 8 is a continuing controversial issue in specific claims or treaty rights litigation. It is important to remember that Mair's interpretation and understanding of the events surrounding the treaty negotiations is merely one perspective. Nevertheless, the reprint will be a readily available source for the interpretation of Treaty No. 8 and the negotiations that took place.

One ought to be a somewhat critical when reading Mair. It must be remembered that sometimes "facts don't speak for themselves."[20] Someone must interpret those facts. Each person has their own interpretation of a specific occurrence based on their background, culture, biases, and perception.[21] Mair had his own biases colouring his interpretation. For example, he was an ardent nationalist and patriot. He also "represented to an extreme the contemptuous Upper Canadian dismissal of the Métis claims."[22] He also agitated for the full force of the state to suppress the uprising. During the 1885 Métis and First Nation uprising, he was an officer in the militia, more specifically, the Governor-General's Body Guard.[23] He had prepared a work called "The Conquest of Canada" and wrote a series of papers for the Montreal *Gazette* entitled "Canada in the Far West"[24] that reflected his stance as a promoter of Canadian imperial expansion into the Northwest. W.L. Morton described Mair's presence in the North-West Territories as "an agent of Canadian manifest destiny."[25] Mair also "knew and represented those elements in English Canada which saw Confederation as preparation for and prelude to the expansion of the new Dominion to the Rockies and the Pacific."[26] He was a believer in progress and development, and his descriptions of the Treaty 8 territory are filled with speculation of the agricultural or forestry value of the land. In fact, Mair was a speculator himself who would profit from increased settlement of the west.[27] It is questionable that someone with these beliefs would or could interpret the events surrounding the treaty negotiations and scrip taking without some form of prejudice.

Mair was also very much an upper class English Canadian who viewed Europeans as superior to "primitive" peoples. Morton wrote of Mair's attitude, "Cheery, confident, cocky,

Charlie Mair, a blond, stocky Anglo-Saxon, was a self-commissioned apostle of the higher civilization of old Canada."[28] Mair merely reflected a prevalent attitude of the time.[29] He had an image of First Nation persons as the "noble savage" and showed his disappointment when he met some who looked "civilized" in appearance.[30] Mair also had the preconceived notion that the First Nations would ultimately disappear.[31] Therefore, to him, as well as to the new Dominion of Canada policy-makers, "the native peoples and their lands of the West were regarded mainly as obstacles to expansion."[32] Mair describes certain Métis or First Nations persons who were critical of the treaty as "agitators" and their impact as "evil effects."[33] Mair's background and biases are reflected throughout his book.

Historically, First Nations had a specific relationship with the European fur traders.[34] This relationship of equality and respect would have coloured their perception and understanding of what the treaty negotiations were to be. Ceremonies, gift giving, and speech making gave the event the air of solemnity and significance. The First Nations leaders were strong negotiators. They may have had little choice but to accept the treaty, but they pressed hard for their concerns to be met, especially relating to their traditional livelihood and education for their children.[35] The Commissioners continually reminded them of the continued encroachment of White settlers who would take up their traditional lands. They had previously encountered severe food shortages during some winters. With the gold rush and the encroachment of White and Métis trappers, they also felt they needed the protection of the laws. It is within this context and background that Mair should be read.

This reprint of *Through the Mackenzie Basin* should be useful to anyone interested in the history and development of north-western Canada. It should be read by many citizens of Canada so that they might better understand why First Nations hold the view they do regarding the treaties. I welcome this reprint and hope it reaches a wide readership.

Brian Calliou

Notes

1. See for example John Goddard, *Last Stand of the Lubicon Cree* (Vancouver: Douglas and McIntyre, 1991); Thomas Flanagan, "Some Factors Bearing on the Origins of the Lubicon Lake Dispute 1899–1940" in *Alberta* 2, no. 2 (1990): 47.
2. Charles Mair, *Through the Mackenzie Basin* (Toronto: William Briggs, 1908), p. 67.
3. Ibid., p. 15.
4. Richard Davis, "Presentation: Treaty 8 Perspectives on Consultation Policies and Practices" to *The Duty to Consult Aboriginal People: Implications for Resource Development on Traditional Lands in Alberta*, a workshop held by the Canadian Institute of Resources Law and the Arctic Institute of North America at Calgary, Alberta, 8 June 1998.
5. Rene Fumoleau, *As Long As This Land Shall Last: A History of Treaty 8 and Treaty 11, 1870 to 1939* (Toronto: McClelland and Stewart, 1973).
6. Richard Daniel, "The Spirit and Terms of Treaty Eight" in Richard T. Price, ed., *The Spirit of the Alberta Indian Treaties* (Edmonton: Pica Pica Press, 1987); see also Richard Daniel, "Indian Rights and Hinterland Resources: The Case of Northern Alberta" Masters Thesis, Department of Sociology, University of Alberta, 1977.
7. Dennis Madill, *Treaty Research Report: Treaty Eight* (Ottawa: Treaty and Historical Research Centre, Indian and Northern Affairs, 1986).
8. Bennett McCardle, *The Rules of the Game: The Development of Government Controls Over Indian Hunting and Trapping in Treaty Eight (Alberta) to 1930* (Ottawa: Treaty and Aboriginal Rights Research, Indian Association of Alberta, 1976).
9. Richard T. Price, *Legacy: Indian Treaty Relationships* (Edmonton: Plains Publishing, 1991); see also Richard T. Price and Shirleen Smith, "Treaty 8 and Traditional Livelihoods: Historical and Contemporary Perspectives" in *Native Studies Review* 9, no. 1 (1993–1994): 51.
10. John W. Chalmers, "Treaty No. 8," in John W. Chalmers, *Laird of the West* (Calgary: Detselig Enterprises Ltd., 1981), p. 211.
11. David W. Leonard, *Delayed Frontier: The Peace River Country to 1909* (Calgary: Detselig Enterprises Ltd., 1995).
12. Ibid., p. 19.
13. Chalmers, *Laird of the West*, p. 225.
14. John W. Garvin, ed., "Editor's Foreword," in Charles Mair, *Tecumseh, a Drama and Canadian Poems* (Toronto: The Radisson Society of Canada, 1926), p. vi.
15. Ibid.

16. Douglas Sanders, "The Queen's Promises" in Louis Knafla, ed., *Law and Justice in a New Land: Essays in Western Canadian Legal History* (Toronto: Carswell, 1986).

17. Leonard I. Rotman, "Taking Aim at the Canons of Treaty Interpretation in Canadian Aboriginal Rights Jurisprudence," *University of New Brunswick Law Journal* 46 (1997): 11. Rotman explains that the Supreme Court of Canada has developed principles of law that provide for a liberal and generous interpretation of treaties with any ambiguities to be decided in favour of the First Nations. The recent Supreme Court of Canada decision in *Delgamuukw* [1998] 1 *Canadian Native Law Reporter* 14 held that all courts must give serious consideration and weight to the oral traditions of First Nations.

18. Richard Davis, Presentation; also stated by Charlie Chissakay, Panel Discussion, *The Duty to Consult Aboriginal People: Implications for Resource Development on Traditional Lands in Alberta*, a workshop held by the Canadian Institute of Resources Law and the Arctic Institute of North America at Calgary, Alberta, 8 June 1998.

19. Chief Charlie Desjarlais, Panel Discussion *The Duty to Consult Aboriginal People: Implications for Resource Development on Traditional Lands in Alberta*, a workshop held by the Canadian Institute of Resources Law and the Arctic Institute of North America at Calgary, Alberta, 8 June 1998.

20. Harold D. Woodman, "Do Facts Speak for Themselves? Writing the Historical Essay," *Perspectives* (December 1987).

21. For example, Julie Cruikshank, "Invention of Anthropology in British Columbia's Supreme Court: Oral Tradition as Evidence in Delgamuukw v. B.C." in *BC Studies*, Special Issue, no. 95 (1992): 25, argues that anthropologists and ethnohistorians are becoming more critical of the written document and are more aware of the ethnocentric bias in western documents and viewing documents within the context in which they were written.

22. Dennis Duffy, "Charles Mair" in *The Canadian Encyclopaedia* (2nd Edition), Vol. II (Edmonton: Hurtig Publishers, 1988), p. 1287.

23. W. Stewart Wallace, "Charles Mair" in W. Stewart Wallace, ed., *The Dictionary of Canadian Biography* (Toronto: MacMillan Co., 1945), p. 435.

24. Henry James Morgan, "Charles Mair" in Henry James Morgan, ed., *The Canadian Men and Women of the Time: A Handbook of Canadian Biography*, 1st Edition (Toronto: William Briggs, 1898).

25. W.L. Morton, "Two Young Men, 1869: Charles Mair and Louis Riel" in *Transactions of the Historical and Scientific Society of Manitoba*, Vol. 30 (1973–74), p. 34.

26. Ibid., p. 34

27. Robert Norwood, "Introduction" in Charles Mair, *Tecumseh, a Drama and Other Canadian Poems*, p. xxiv; see also Morton, "Two Young Men," p. 41, where he states, "Mair was the innocent and thoughtless champion of the land rush and the speculators. He indeed was to become a modest speculator himself in the Portage la Prairie he had praised so highly as the path of empire."

28. Ibid., p. 33.

29. See for example, R.G. Moyles and Doug Owram, "Specimens of a Dying Race: British Views of the Canadian Indian" in R.G. Moyles and Doug Owram, *Imperial Dreams and Colonial Realities: British Views of Canada, 1880–1914* (Toronto: University of Toronto Press, 1988); for a more general analysis, see also Daniel Francis, *The Imaginary Indian: The Image of the Indian in Canadian Culture* (Vancouver: Arsenal Pulp Press, 1992).

30. Mair, *Through the Mackenzie Basin*, pp. 54–55.

31. Ibid., p. 88, where Mair states that the name "Peace River" was given by the French "which we have adopted, and by this name the river will doubtless be known when the Indians, whose home it has been for ages, have disappeared."

32. Gary Kelly, "Class, Race, and Cultural Revolution: Treaties and the Making of Western Canada" in *Alberta* 1, no. 2 (1989): 27.

33. Mair, *Through the Mackenzie Basin*, p. 53.

34. Price and Smith, "Treaty 8 and Traditional Livelihoods," pp. 54–55.

35. Mair, *Through the Mackenzie Basin*, pp. 59–63.

ANNOTATIONS

1. **Page 27, line 2**—J.A. Côté should not be confused with Jean L. Côté, the surveyor and later MLA and Senator from Grouard.

2. **Page 31, line 26**—"Tawutinaw" is today spelled "Tawatinaw." This valley was the site of the cannibalism of the Cree, Swift Runner, upon members of his family during 1878–79, for which he was found guilty of murder and hanged.

3. **Page 54, second paragraph**—Most non-natives were bankers and traders from Edmonton, many interested in the purchase of scrip. Among those identified by the Edmonton *Bulletin* were Charles Alloway, Stanislas LaRue, J.H. Picard, Richard Secord, Fletcher Bredin, G.R.F. Kirkpatrick, Colin Fraser, Henry Burbank and Michael McDermott. Also present was James Cornwall, while those arriving shortly thereafter would include Twelve-Foot Davis, John Norris, Dan Carey, Thomas Atkinson, Clem Paul, and Fred and Allie Brick. See the *Bulletin* for 26 June and 10 July 1899. Missionaries included the Oblates Bishop Grouard and Father Lacombe; and the Anglican Reverends D.G. White, W.G. White and George Holmes. Holmes's correspondence to Bishop Richard Young provides the most revealing detail of the events of 1899 at Lesser Slave Lake from the point of view of a missionary. See Provincial Archives of Alberta, Anglican Diocese of Athabasca Records, A/281.

4. **Page 55, last paragraph**—For the Edmonton *Bulletin's* account of these proceedings, see this paper for 17 and 26 June, and 6 July 1899. It was the position of the *Bulletin* (17 June) that, on the eve of the negotiations, "the Chiefs are all in favour of the treaty."

5. **Page 65, first paragraph**—The initial schedule for the Commissioners had called for appointments at Lesser Slave Lake (8 June), Peace River Crossing (13 June), Fort Dunvegan (16 June), Fort St. John (21 June), Fort Vermilion (29 June), Red River Post (3 July), Fort Chipewyan (8 July), Fort Smith (14 July), Fond du Lac (24 July), Fort McMurray (4 August), Wabasca (16 August), and Athabasca Landing (23 August). Overall, the Commissions were regularly between two and three weeks behind schedule.

6. **Page 66, line 10**—"Wahpooskow" is today known as "Wabasca."

7. **Page 66, line 14**—"1889" should read "1899."

8. **Page 68, first paragraph**—For its analysis of the scrip issue, see the Edmonton *Bulletin* for 15 May and 1 June 1899. Frank Oliver's speeches in Parliament on the subject were reported in the *Bulletin* on 29 May and 24 July 1899.

9. **Page 68, line 23**—See above, Annotation #3. Of these, Charles Alloway and Richard Secord travelled with the Scrip Commissioners to Peace River Crossing, where the purchase price was as high as $130 per $240 scrip note. See the Edmonton *Bulletin*, 25 September 1899.

10. **Page 72, line 16**—"Calahaisen" is today spelt "Calahasen."

11. **Page 76, line 6**—"Pahayo" is spelt in the court records as "Pay-i-uu." See this case as heard in the Edmonton Court House in Provincial Archives of Alberta, 79.266 (North Alberta Judicial District Court Records) No. 157. See also the Edmonton *Bulletin*, 14 August 1899.

12. **Page 76, line 8**—"Weeghteko" is otherwise spelt as "Whitego," and known on the southern prairies in Cree as "Windego."

13. **Page 89, line 1**—"Trappers and traders" should read "trippers and traders."

14. **Page 89, line 14**—"Mr C. Brymmer" was actually, "Charles Bremner."

15. **Page 89, line 23**—"Pooscapee's Prairie" was then and now known as the "Pouce Coupé Prairie," which surrounds Dawson Creek, British Columbia. It was named after a Beaver chief whose ancestor of the same name is mentioned in the journal of Simon Fraser of 1806.

16. **Page 90, line 1**—"Father Busson" was actually, Father Auguste "Husson."

17. **Page 90, line 9**—Thomas Allen Brick would be the first Member of the Provincial Parliament for the Peace River riding in 1906.

18. **Page 117**—The "Fort Resolution" mentioned here was actually, "Fort Enterprise."

THROUGH THE MACKENZIE BASIN

A Narrative of the Athabasca and Peace River
Treaty Expedition of 1899

BY

CHARLES MAIR

English Secretary of the Half-breed Commission ; Author of
" Tecumseh : a Drama," Etc.

With a Map of the Country Ceded and Numerous Photographs of
Native Life and Scenery

———————

TORONTO
WILLIAM BRIGGS
1908

Hon. David Laird
Ex-Lieut.-Governor N.W.T. Leader of the Treaty Expedition of 1899

TO

Ꮯhe Ꮒon. David Laird

LEADER OF
THE TREATY EXPEDITION OF 1899

THIS RECORD IS

CORDIALLY INSCRIBED

BY HIS OLD FRIEND

THE AUTHOR

PREFACE

THE literature descriptive of Northern Canada, from the days of Hearne and Mackenzie to those of Tyrrell and Hanbury, is by no means scanty. A copious bibliography might be compiled of the records of its exploration with a view to trade, science, or sport, particularly in recent years; whilst the accounts of the search for Sir John Franklin furnish no inconsiderable portion of such productions in the past. These books are more or less available in our Public Libraries, and, at any rate, do not enter into consideration here. Such records, however, furnished almost our sole knowledge of the Northern Territories until the year 1888, when the first earnest effort of the Canadian Parliament was made " to inquire into the resources of the great Mackenzie Basin."

Through the instrumentality of the late Sir John Schultz, then a Senator, a Select Committee of the Senate was appointed for that purpose. Sir John had always taken a great interest in the question, and was Chairman of the Committee which took evidence, oral and by letter, from a great many persons who possessed more or less knowledge of the regions in question. The evidence was voluminous, and the reader who lacks access to the Blue Book containing it will find the gist of the Report in the Appendix to this volume.

A treaty with the Indians of the region followed this Report in 1899; but, owing to the absence of roads and markets, and other essentials of civilized life, not to speak of the vast unsettled areas of prairie to the south, the incoming, until now that railways are projected, of any great body of immigrants was very wisely discouraged, and this in the interest of the settler himself. The following narrative, therefore, has lain in the author's diary since the year of the expedition it records, its publication having been unavoidably delayed. It is now given to the public with the assurance that, whilst he does not claim freedom from error, which would be absurd, he took pains with it on the spot, and can vouch, at all events, for its general accuracy.

The writer, and doubtless some of his readers, can recall the time when to go to " Peace River " seemed almost like going to another sphere, where, it was conjectured, life was lived very differently from that of civilized man. And, truly, it was to enter into an unfamiliar state of things; a region in which a primitive people, not without faults or depravities, lived on Nature's food, and throve on her unfailing harvest of fur. A region in which they often left their beaver, silver fox or marten packs—the envy of Fashion—lying by the dog-trail, or hanging to some sheltering tree, because no one stole, and took their fellow's word without question, because no one lied. A very simple folk indeed, in whose language profanity was unknown, and who had no desire to leave their congenital solitudes for any other spot on earth: solitudes which so charmed the educated minds who brought the white man's religion, or traffic, to their doors, that, like the Lotus-eaters, they, too, felt little craving to depart. Yet they were not regions of sloth or idleness, but of necessary toil; of the laborious chase and the endless activities of aboriginal life: the region of a people familiar with its fauna and flora—of skilled but unconscious naturalists, who knew no science.

Such was the state of society in that remote land in its golden age; before the enterprising " free-trader " brought with him the first-fruits of the Tree of Knowledge; long before the half-crazed gold-hunters rushed upon the scene, the " Klondikers " from the saloons and music-halls of New York and Chicago, to whom the incredible honesty of the natives, the absence of money, and the strange barter in skins (the wyan or aghti of the Indian) seemed like a phantasmagoria—an existence utterly removed from " real " life—

that ostentatious and vulgar world in which they longed to play a part. It was this inroad which led to the entrance of the authority of the Queen—the Kitchi Okemasquay—not so much to preserve order, where, without the law, the natives had not unwisely governed themselves, as to prepare them for the incoming world, and to protect them from a new aggressor with whom their rude tribunals were incompetent to deal. To this end the Expedition of 1899 was sent by Government to treat for the transfer of their territorial rights, to ascertain, as well, the numbers and holdings of the few white or other settlers who had made a start at farming or stock-raising within its borders, and to clear the way for the incoming tide of settlement when the time became ripe for its extension to the North. This time is rapidly approaching, and when it comes the primitive life and methods of travel depicted will pass away forever. It is important, therefore, that as many descriptive records as possible, and at first-hand, should be preserved. Though the following account is but one of many experiences in remote Athabasca, it may claim some special value as a record of the Great Treaty by which that vast territory was ceded to the Crown; a territory equal in area to a group of European kingdoms or of American states, and whose resources, as yet comparatively unknown, are arousing eager surmise and conjecture in all directions.

Whilst putting on record the methods and hardships of travel during a singularly adverse season, the negotiations with the Indians and half-breeds, and the superficial features of the country passed through, the writer was also aware of the fact that much information of great scientific value regarding the fauna of the North, collected by his friend, Roderick MacFarlane, Esq., for many years a chief-factor of the Hudson's Bay Company, had been hitherto withheld from the general public. This keen observer's " Notes on Mammals, with Remarks on Explorers and Explorations of

the Far North " was an important contribution to the
Archives of the Smithsonian Institution (United States
National Museum) ; and his " Notes on and List of Birds
and Eggs Collected in Arctic America," if not exhaustive,
was a similarly valuable addition to its records. It seemed
to the writer very desirable that this information, hidden
away in the " Proceedings " of a foreign scientific institution, should be given to the Canadian public, and, by Mr.
MacFarlane's kind consent and wish, he is now enabled, with
pleasure to himself and profit to his readers, to connect it
with his own narrative of the Treaty Expedition of 1899.

The author has tried to make his narrative not merely an
official record, but interesting as an itinerary, and to impart
to it something of the novelty and fervour of his own sensations at the time. Notwithstanding its shortcomings in these
respects, it may yet be of service in attracting to the remarkable regions described the pioneer who is not afraid of toil,
or the traveller who loves the unprofaned sanctities of
Nature.

CONTENTS

INTRODUCTION

CHAPTER I.

FROM EDMONTON TO LESSER SLAVE LAKE.

CHAPTER II.

LESSER SLAVE RIVER AND LESSER SLAVE LAKE.

CHAPTER III.

TREATY AT LESSER SLAVE LAKE.

CHAPTER IV.

THE HALF-BREED SCRIP COMMISSION.

CHAPTER V.

RESOURCES OF LESSER SLAVE LAKE REGION.

CHAPTER VI.

ON THE TRAIL TO PEACE RIVER.

CHAPTER VII.

DOWN THE PEACE RIVER.

CHAPTER VIII.

FORT CHIPEWYAN TO FORT M'MURRAY.

12 CONTENTS

CHAPTER IX.

THE ATHABASCA RIVER REGION.

CHAPTER X.

THE TRIP TO WAHPOOSKOW.

ILLUSTRATIONS

INTRODUCTION

The important events of A.D. 1857, and the negotiations which led
to the Transfer of the Hudson's Bay Territories—Former
Treaties and the Treaty Commission of 1899.

THE terms upon which Canada obtained her great posses-
sions in the West are generally known, and much has been
written regarding the tentative steps by which, after long
years of waiting, she acquired them. The distinctively prairie,
or southern, portion of the country and its outliers, consti-
tuting " Prince Rupert's Land," had been claimed by the
Hudson's Bay Company since May, 1670, as an absolute
freehold. This and the North-West Territories, in which,
under terminable lease from the Crown, the Company exer-
cised, as in British Columbia, exclusive rights to trade only,
were, as the reader knows, transferred to Canada by Imperial
sanction at the same time. It is not the author's intention,
therefore, to cumber his pages with trite or irrelevant matter;
yet certain transactions which preceded this primordial and
greatest treaty of all not unfittingly may be set forth, though
in the briefest way, as a pardonable introduction to the
following record.

The year 1857 was an eventful one in the annals of " The
North-West," the name by which the Territories were generally known in Canada.* In that year two expeditions

---

*An important event in Red River was begot of the stirring inci-
dents of this year, namely, the starting at Fort Garry, in December,
1859, by two gentlemen from Canada, Messrs. Buckingham and
Caldwell, of the first newspaper printed in British territory east
of British Columbia and west of Lake Superior. It was called the
Nor'-Wester, but, having few advertisements, and only a limited
circulation, the originators sold out to Dr. (afterwards Sir John)
Schultz, who, at his own expense, published the paper, almost down
to the Transfer, as an advocate of Canadian annexation, immigration
and development.

were set afoot to explore the country; one in charge of
Captain Palliser,* equipped by the Imperial Government,
and the other, under Professor Hind, at the expense of the
Government of Canada. An influential body of Red River
settlers, too, at this time petitioned the Canadian Parliament
to extend to the North-West its government and protection;
and in the same year the late Chief Justice Draper was sent
to England to challenge the validity of the Hudson's Bay
Company's charter, and to urge the opening up of the country
for settlement. But, above all, a committee of the British
House of Commons took evidence that year upon all sorts of
questions concerning the North-West, and particularly its
suitability for settlement, much of which was valueless owing
to its untruth. Nevertheless, the Imperial Committee, after
weighing all the evidence, reported that the Territories were
fit for settlement, and that it was desirable that Canada
should annex them, and hoped that the Government would be
enabled to bring in a bill to that end at the next session of
Parliament. Five years later, the Duke of Newcastle, who
became Secretary of State for the Colonies in 1859, and
accompanied the Prince of Wales to Canada as official
adviser in 1860, having in his possession the petition of the
Red River settlers, as printed by order of the Canadian
Legislature, brought the matter up in a vigorous speech in
the House of Lords, in which he expressed his belief that
the Hudson's Bay Company's charter was invalid, though,
he added, " it would be a serious blow to the rights of property to meddle with a charter two hundred years old. But it
might happen," he continued, " in the inevitable course of

---

*Strange to say, Captain Palliser reported that he considered a
line of communication entirely through British territory, connecting the Eastern Provinces and British Columbia, out of the question,
as the Astronomical Boundary adopted isolated the prairie country
from Canada. Professor Hind, on the other hand, in the same year,
standing on an eminence on the Qu'Appelle, beheld in imagination
the smoke of the locomotive ascending from the train speeding over
the prairies on its way through Canada from the Atlantic to the
Pacific.

events, that Parliament would be asked to annul even such
a charter as this, in order, as set forth in the Queen's Speech,
that all obstacles to an unbroken chain of loyal settlements,
stretching from ocean to ocean, should be removed." British
Columbia, which had become a Province in 1858, was now
urging the Imperial Government with might and main to
furnish a waggon-road and telegraph line to connect her, not
only with the Territories and Canada, but with the United
Empire. She was met by the stiffest of opposition, the
opposition of a very old corporation strongly entrenched in
the governing circles of both parties. But the clamour of
British Columbia was in the air, and her suggestions, hotly
opposed by the Company, had been brought before the House
of Lords by another peer. In the discussion which followed,
the Duke of Newcastle declared that " it seemed monstrous
that any body of gentlemen should exercise fee-simple rights
which precluded the future colonization of that territory, as
well as the opening of lines of communication through it."
The Minister's idea at the time seemed to be to cancel the
charter, and to concede proprietary rights around fur posts
only, together with a certain money payment, considerably
less, it appears, than what was ultimately agreed upon.

The Hudson's Bay Company, alarmed at the outlook and
the attitude of the Colonial Secretary, offered their entire
interests and belongings, trade and territorial, to the Imperial
Government for a million and a half pounds sterling, an offer
which the Duke was disposed to accept, but which was unfortunately declined by Mr. Gladstone, then Chancellor of the
Exchequer. The Duke, who had resigned his office in 1864,
died in October following, and in the meantime a change of
a startling character had come over the time-honoured company, which sold out to a new company in 1863, being
merged into, or rather merging into itself, an organization
known as " The Anglo-International Financial Association,"
which included several prominent American capitalists. The
old name was retained, but everything else was to be changed.

The policy of exclusion was to cease, immigration was to be encouraged, and a telegraph line built through the Territories to the Pacific coast. The wire for this was actually shipped, and lay in Rupert's Land for years, until made use of by the Mackenzie Administration in the building of the Government telegraph line, which followed the railway route defined by Sir Sandford Fleming. The old Hudson's Bay Company's shares, of a par value of half a million pounds sterling, were increased to a million and a half under the new adjustment, and were thrown upon the market in shares of twenty pounds sterling each. Sir Edmund Head, an old ex-Governor of Canada, was made Governor of the new company. The Stock Exchange was not altogether favourable, and the remaining shares were only sold in the Winnipeg land boom of 1881.

The alien element in the new company seemed to inspire the politicians of the United States with surpassing hopes and ideas. An offer to purchase its territorial interests was made in January, 1866, by American capitalists, which was not unfavourably glanced at by the directorate. It was capped later on. The corollary of the proposal was a bill, actually introduced into the United States Congress in July following, and read twice, " providing for the admission of the States of Nova Scotia, New Brunswick, Canada East and Canada West, and for the organization of the Territories of Selkirk, Saskatchewan and Columbia." The bill provided that " The United States would pay ten millions of dollars to the Hudson's Bay Company in full of all claims to territory or jurisdiction in North America, whether founded on the Charter of the Company, or any treaty, law, or usage." The grandiosity, to use a mild phrase, of such a measure needs no comment. But though it seems amusing to the Canadian of to-day, it was by no means a joke forty years ago. As a matter of fact, the then almost uninhabited Territories, cut off from the centres of Canadian activity by a wilderness of over a thousand miles, would have been invaded by Fenians and filibusters but for the fact that they were a part of the

The Treaty Commission

Seated—Mr. Round, Hon. David Laird, Mr. Young

Standing—Mr. d'Eschambault, two R.N.W.M.P. constables, Camp-Manager McKay and the cook, Lafrance

British Empire. An attempt at this was indeed made at a later date. This possibility was afterwards formulated, evidently as a threat, by Senator Charles Sumner during the "Alabama Claims" discussion, in his astonishing memorandum to Secretary Fish. "The greatest trouble, if not peril," he said, "is from Fenianism, which is excited by the British flag in Canada. Therefore, 'the withdrawal of the British flag' cannot be abandoned as a preliminary of such a settlement as is now proposed. To make the settlement complete the withdrawal should be from this hemisphere, including provinces and islands." A refreshing proposition, truly!

It was the Imperial Government, of course, which figured most prominently throughout the "North-West" question. But, it may be reasonably asked, what was Canada doing, with her deeper interests still, to further them in those long years of discussion and delay? With the exception of the Hind Expedition, the Draper mission, the printing and discussion of the Red River settlers' petition and consequent Commission of Inquiry, certainly not much was done by Parliament. More was done outside than in the House to arouse public interest; for example, the two admirable lectures delivered in Montreal in 1858 by the late Lieutenant-Governor Morris, followed by the powerful advocacy of the Hon. William Macdougall and others, aided by the Toronto *Globe,* a small portion of the Canadian press, and the circulation, limited as it was, of the Red River newspaper, the *Nor'-Wester,* in Ontario.

An unseen, but adverse, parliamentary influence had all along hampered the Cabinet; an influence adverse not only to the acquisition of the Territories, but even to closer connection by railway with the Maritime Provinces.* This sinister influence was only overcome by the great Conferences which resulted in the passage of the British North America Act in 1867, which contained a clause (Article 11, Sec. 146),

Vide a series of articles contributed to the Toronto *Week,* in July, 1896, by Mr. Malcolm McLeod, Q.C., of Ottawa, Ont.

inserted at the instance of Mr. Macdougall, providing for the inclusion of Rupert's Land and the North-West Territories upon terms to be defined in an address to the Queen, and subject to her approval. In pursuance of this clause, Mr. Macdougall in 1867 introduced into the first Parliament of the Dominion a series of eight resolutions, which, after much opposition, were at length passed, and were followed by the embodying address, drafted by a Special Committee of the House, and which was duly transmitted to the Imperial Government. This was followed by the mission of Messrs. Cartier and Macdougall to London, to treat for the transfer of the Territories, which, through the mediation of Lord Granville, was finally effected. The date fixed upon for the transfer was the first of December, 1869. Unfortunately for Lieutenant-Governor Macdougall, owing to the outbreak of armed rebellion at Red River, it was postponed without his knowledge, and it was not until the 15th of July, 1870, that the whole country finally became a part of the Dominion of Canada. With the latter date the annals of Prince Rupert's Land and the North-West Territory end, and the history of Western Canada begins.

But whilst the Hudson's Bay Company's territorial rights and those of Great Britain had been at last transferred to the Dominion, there remained inextinguished the most intrinsic of all, viz., the rights of the Indians and their collaterals to their native and traditional soil. The adjustment of these rights was assumed by the Canadian Parliament in the last but one of the resolutions introduced by Mr. Macdougall, and no time was lost after the transfer in carrying out its terms, " in conformity with the equitable principles which have uniformly governed the Crown in its dealings with the aborigines."*

*In the foregoing brief sketch, the author, for lack of space, omits all reference to the Red River troubles, which preceded the actual transfer, as also to the military expedition under Col. Wolseley, the threatened recall of which from Prince Arthur's Landing, in July, 1870, was blocked by the bold and vigorous action of the Canada First Party in Toronto.

Former Treaties.

Before passing on to my theme, a glance at the treaties made in Manitoba and the organized Territories may be of interest to the unfamiliar reader.

The first treaty, in what is now a part of Manitoba, was made in pursuance of a purchase of the old District of Assiniboia from the Hudson's Bay Company in 1811 by Lord Selkirk, who in that year sent out the first batch of colonists from the north of Scotland to Red River. The Indian title to the land, however, was not conveyed by the Crees and Saulteaux until 1817, when Peguis and others of their chiefs ceded a portion of their territory for a yearly payment of a quantity of tobacco. The ceded tract extended from the mouth of the Red River southward to Grand Forks, and, westward, along the Assiniboine River to Rat Creek, the depth of the reserve being the distance at which a white horse could be seen on the plains, though this matter is not very clear. The British boundary at that time ran south of Red Lake, and would still so run but for the indifference of bygone Commissioners. This purchase became the theatre of Lord Selkirk's far-seeing scheme of British settlement in the North-West, with whose varying fortunes and romantic history the average reader is familiar.

The first Canadian treaties were those effected by Mr. Weemys Simpson in 1871, first at Stone Fort, Man., covering the old purchase from Peguis and others, and a large extent of territory in addition, the stipulated terms of payment being afterwards greatly enlarged. These treaties are known as Nos. 1 and 2, and were followed by the North-West Angle Treaty, effected by Lieutenant-Governor Morris, in 1873, with the Ojibway Saulteaux. In 1874 the Qu'Appelle Treaty, after prolonged discussion and inter-tribal jealousy and disturbance, was concluded by Lieutenant-Governor Morris, the Hon. David Laird, then Minister of the Interior, and Mr. W. J. Christie, of the Hudson's Bay Company.

Treaty No. 5 followed, with the cession of 100,000 square miles of territory, covering the Lake Winnipeg region, etc., after which the Great Treaty (No. 6), at Forts Carlton and Pitt, in 1876, covering almost all the country drained by the two Saskatchewans, was partly effected by Mr. Morris and his associates, the recalcitrants being afterwards induced by Mr. Laird to adhere to the treaty, with the exception of the notorious Big Bear, the insurgent chief who figured so prominently in the Rebellion of 1885. The final treaty, or No. 7, made with the Assiniboines and Blackfeet, the most powerful and predatory of all our Plain Indians, was concluded by Mr. Laird and the late Lieut.-Colonel McLeod in 1877. By this last treaty had now been ceded the whole country from Lake Winnipeg to the Rocky Mountains, and from the international boundary to the District of Athabasca. But there remained in native hands still that vast northern anticlinal, which differs almost entirely in its superficial features from the prairies and plains to the south; and it was this region, enormous in extent and rich in economic resources, which, it was decided by Government, should now be placed by treaty at the disposal of the Canadian people. To this end it was determined that at Lesser Slave Lake the first conference should be held, and the initial steps taken towards the cession of the whole western portion of the unceded territory up to the 60th parallel of north latitude.

The more immediate motive for treating with the Indians of Athabasca has been already referred to, viz., the discovery of gold in the Klondike, and the astonishing rush of miners and prospectors, in consequence, to the Yukon, not only from the Pacific side, but, east of the mountains, by way of the Peace and Mackenzie rivers. Up to that date, excepting to the fur-traders and a few missionaries, settlers, explorers, geologists and sportsmen, the Peace River region was practically unknown; certainly as little known to the people of Ontario, for example, as was the Red River country thirty

Half-breed Scrip Commission

Seated—Major Walker and **Mr.** Coté.   *Standing*—**Mr.** Prudhomme and Mr. Mair.

The Royal North-West Mounted Police Contingent

remote

years before.   It was thought to be a most difficult country
to reach—a *terra incognita*—rude and dangerous, having no
allurements for the average Canadian, whose notions about
it, if he had any, were limited, as usual, to the awe-inspiring
legend of " barbarous Indians and perpetual frost." ——

legend

There is a lust, however, the unquenchable lust for gold,
which seems to arouse the dullest from their apathy.   This
is the *primum mobile;* from earliest days the sensational
mover of civilized man, and not unlikely to remain so until
our old planet capsizes again, and the poles become the
equator with troglodites for inhabitants.   No barriers seem
insurmountable to this rampant spirit; and, urged by it, the
gold-seekers, chiefly aliens from the United States, plunged
into the wilderness of Athabasca without hesitation, and
without as much as " by your leave " to the native.   Some
of these marauders, as was to be expected, exhibited on the
way a congenital contempt for the Indian's rights.   At various
places his horses were killed, his dogs shot, his bear-traps
broken up.   An outcry arose in consequence, which inevitably
would have led to reprisals and bloodshed had not the Government stepped in and forestalled further trouble by a
prompt recognition of the native's title.   Hitherto he had
been content with his lot in these remote wildernesses, and
well might he be!   One of the vast river systems of the Continent, perhaps the greatest of them all, considering the area
drained, teeming with fish, and alive with fur and antler,
was his home—a region which furnished him in abundance
with the means of life, not to speak of such surplus of lux-
uries as was brought to his doors by his old and paternal
friend, " John Company."   His wants were simple, his life
healthy, though full of toil, his appetite great—an appetite
which throve upon what it fed, and gave rise to fabulous
feats of eating, recalling the exploits of the beloved and big-
bellied Ben of nursery lore.

But the spirit of change was brooding even here.   The

moose, the beaver and the bear had for years been decreasing, and other fur-bearing animals were slowly but surely lessening with them. The natives, aware of this, were now alive, as well, to concurrent changes foreign to their experience. Recent events had awakened them to a sense of the value the white man was beginning to place upon their country as a great storehouse of mineral and other wealth, enlivened otherwise by the sensible decrease of their once unfailing resources. These events were, of course, the Government borings for petroleum, the formation of parties to prospect, with a view to developing, the minerals of Great Slave Lake, but, above all, the inroad of gold-seekers by way of Edmonton. The latter was viewed with great mistrust by the Indians, the outrages referred to showing, like straws in the wind, the inevitable drift of things had the treaties been delayed. For, as a matter of fact, those now peaceable tribes, soured by lawless aggression, and sheltered by their vast forests, might easily have taken an Indian revenge, and hampered, if not hindered, the safe settlement of the country for years to come. The Government, therefore, decided to treat with them at once on equitable terms, and to satisfy their congeners, the half-breeds, as well, by an issue of scrip certificates such as their fellows had already received in Manitoba and the organized Territories. To this end adjustments were made by the Hon. Clifford Sifton, then Minister of the Interior and Superintendent-General of Indian Affairs, during the winter of 1898-9, and a plan of procedure and basis of treatment adopted, the carrying out of which was placed in the hands of a double Commission, one to frame and effect the Treaty, and secure the adhesion of the various tribes, and the other to investigate and extinguish the half-breed title. At the head of the former was placed the Hon. David Laird, a gentleman of wide experience in the early days in the North-West Territories, whose successful treaty with the refractory Blackfeet and their

allies is but one of many evidences of his tact and sagacity.*
A nature in which fairness and firmness met was, of all dis-
positions, the most suited to handle such important negotiations with the Indians as parting with their blood-right.
Fortunately these qualities were pre-eminent in Mr. Laird,
who had administered the government of the organized Territories, at a primitive stage in their history, in the wisest
manner, and, at the close of his official career, returned to
his home in Prince Edward Island leaving not an enemy
behind him.

The other Treaty Commissioners were the Hon. James
Ross, Minister of Public Works in the Territorial Government, and Mr. J. A. McKenna, then private secretary
to the Superintendent-General of Indian Affairs, and
who had been for some years a valued officer of the Indian
Department. With them was associated, in an advisory
capacity, the Rev. Father Lacombe, O.M.I., Vicar-General
of St. Albert, Alta., whose history had been identified for
fifty years with the Canadian North-West, and whose career
had touched the currents of primitive life at all points.†

---

*The Hon. David Laird is a native of Prince Edward Island. His
father emigrated from Scotland to that Province early in the last
century, and ultimately became a member of its Executive Council.
After leaving college his son David began life as a journalist, but
later on took to politics, and being called, like his father, to the
Executive Council, was selected as one of the delegates to Ottawa to
arrange for the entrance of the Island into the Canadian Confederation. He was subsequently elected to the Dominion House of Commons, and became Minister of the Interior in the Mackenzie
Administration. After three years' occupancy of this department
he was made Lieut.-Governor of the North-West Territories, an office
which he filled without bias and to the satisfaction of both the foes
and friends of his own party. He returned to the Island at the close
of his official term, but was called thence by the Laurier Administration to take charge of Indian affairs in the West, with residence in
Winnipeg, which is now his permanent home.

†Father Lacombe is by birth a French Canadian, his native parish
being St. Sulpice, in the Island of Montreal, where he was born in
the year 1827. On the mother's side he is said to draw his descent
from the daughter of a habitant on the St. Lawrence River called
Duhamel, who was stolen in girlhood by the Ojibway Indians, and
subsequently taken to wife by their chief, to whom she bore two
sons. By mere accident, her uncle, who was one of a North-West

Not associated with the Commission, but travelling with it as a guest, was the Right Rev. E. Grouard, O.M.I., the Roman Catholic Bishop of Athabasca and Mackenzie rivers, who was returning, after a visit to the East, to his headquarters at Fort Chipewyan, where his influence and knowledge of the language, it was believed, would be of great service when the treaty came under consideration there. The secretaries of the Commission were Mr. Harrison Young, a son-in-law of the Rev. George McDougall, the distinguished missionary who perished so unaccountably on the plains in the winter of 1876, and Mr. J. W. Martin, an agreeable young gentleman from Goderich, Ont. Connected with the party in an advisory capacity, like Father Lacombe, and as interpreter, was Mr. Pierre d'Eschambault, who had been for over thirty years an officer in the Hudson's Bay Company's service. The camp-manager was Mr. Henry McKay, of an old and highly esteemed North-West family. Such was the *personnel,* official and informal, of the Treaty Commission, to which was also attached Mr. H. A. Conroy, as accountant, robust and genial, and well fitted for the work.

The Half-breed Scrip Commission, whose duties began where the treaty work ended, was composed of Major Walker, a retired officer of the Royal North-West Mounted Police, who had seen much service in the Territories and was in com-

Company trading party on Lake Huron, met her at an Indian camp on one of the Manitoulin islands, and having identified her as his niece, restored her and her children to her family. Father Lacombe was ordained a priest by Bishop Bourget, of Montreal, and in 1849 set out for Red River, where he became intimately associated with the French half-breeds, accompanying them on their great buffalo hunts, and ministering not only to the spiritual but to the temporal welfare of them and their descendants down to the present day. In 1851 he took charge of the Lake Ste. Anne Mission, and subsequently of St. Albert, the first house in which he helped to build; and from these Missions he visited numbers of outlying regions, including Lesser Slave Lake. His principal missionary work, however, for twenty years was pursued amongst the Blackfeet Indians on the Great Plains, during which he witnessed many a perilous onslaught in the constant warfare between them and their traditional enemies, the Crees. Being now over eighty years of age, he has retired from active duty, and is spending the remainder of his days at Pincher Creek, Alta., where, it is understood, he is preparing his memoirs for publication at an early date.

mand of the force present at the making of the Fort Carlton Treaty in 1876; and Mr. J. A. Coté, an experienced officer of the Land Department at Ottawa. The secretaries were Mr. J. F. Prudhomme, of St. Boniface, Man., and the writer.

Our transport arrangements, from start to finish, had been placed entirely in the hands of a competent officer of the Hudson's Bay Company, Mr. H. B. Round, an old resident of Athabasca; and to the Commission was also annexed a young medical man, Dr. West, a native of Devonshire, England, whose services were appreciated in a region where doctors were almost unknown. But not the least important and effective constituent of the party was the detachment of the Royal North-West Mounted Police, which joined us at Edmonton, minus their horses, of course; picked men from a picked force; sterling fellows, whose tenacity and hard work in the tracking-harness did yeoman service in many a serious emergency. This detachment consisted of Inspector Snyder, Sergeant Anderson, Corporals Fitzgerald and McClelland, and Constables McLaren, Lett, Burman, Lelonde, Burke, Vernon and Kerr. The conduct of these men, it is needless to say, was the admiration of all, and assisted materially, as will be seen hereafter, in the successful progress of the expedition.

Whilst it had been decided that the proposed adjustments should be effected, if possible, upon the same terms as the previous treaties, it was known that certain changes would be necessary owing to the peculiar topographic features of the country itself. For example, in much of it arable reserves, such as many of the tribes retained in the south, were unavailable, and special stipulations were necessary, in such case, so that there should be no inequality of treatment. But where good land could be had, a novel choice was offered, by which individual Indians, if they wished, could take their inalienable shares in severalty, rather than be subject to the " band," whereby many industrious Indians elsewhere had been greatly hampered in their efforts to improve their condition. But, barring such departures as these, the proposed treaties were to be effected, as I have said, according to precedent. The Commission, then, resting its arguments on the good faith and honour of the Government and people of Canada in the past, looked forward with confidence to a successful treaty in Athabasca, the record of travel and intercourse, to that end, beginning with the following narrative.

Commissioners McKenna and Ross and
Inspector Snyder. R.N.W.M.P.

The venerable missionary, Père Lacombe,
and Commissioner Cote

Athabasca Landing in 1899

Through the Mackenzie Basin

CHAPTER I.

FROM EDMONTON TO LESSER SLAVE LAKE.

Mr. Laird, with his staff, left Winnipeg for Edmonton by the Canadian Pacific express on the 22nd of May, two of the Commissioners having preceded him to that point. The train was crowded, as usual, with immigrants, tourists, globe-trotters and way-passengers. Parties for the Klondike, for California or Japan—once the far East, but now the far West to us—for anywhere and everywhere, a C. P. R. express train carrying the same variety of fortunates and unfortunates as the ocean-cleaving hull. Calgary was reached at one a.m. on the Queen's birthday, and the same morning we left for Edmonton by the C. & E. Railway. Every one was impressed favourably by the fine country lying between these two cities, its intermediate towns and villages, and fast-growing industries. But one thing especially was not overlooked, viz., the honour due to our venerable Queen, alas, so soon to be taken from us.

In the evening we arrived at Strathcona, and found it thronged with people celebrating the day. Crossing the river to Edmonton, we got rooms with some difficulty in one of its crowded hotels, but happily awoke next morning refreshed and ready to view the town. It is needless to describe what has been so often described. Enough to say Edmonton is one of the doors to the great North, an outfitter of its traders, an emporium of its furs. And there is some-

thing more to be said. It has an old fort, or, rather, portions of one, for the vandalism which has let disappear
another, and still more historic, stronghold, is manifest here
as well. And truly, what savage scenes have been enacted
on this very spot! What strife in the days of the rival companies! Edmonton is a city still marked by the fine savour
of the " Old-Timers," who meet once a year to renew asso-
ciations, and for some fleeting but glorious hours recall the
past on the great river. Age is thinning them out, and by
and by the remainder man will shake his " few, sad, last
gray hairs," and slip out, too. But the tradition of him, it
is to be hoped, will live, and bind his memory forever to
the soil he trod, when all this Western world was a wilderness, each primitive settlement a happy family, each unit an
unsophisticated, hospitable soul.

To our mortification we found that our supplies, season-
ably shipped at Winnipeg, would not arrive for several days;
a delay, to begin with, which seemed to prefigure all our
subsequent hindrances. Then rain set in, and it was the
afternoon of the 29th before Mr. Round could get us off.
Once under way, however, with our thirteen waggons, there
was no trouble save from their heavy loads, which could not
be moved faster than a walk. Our first camp was at Sturgeon River—the Namáo Sepe of the Crees—a fine stream
in a defile of hills clothed with poplar and spruce, the former not quite in leaf, for the spring was backward, though
seeding and growth in the Edmonton District was much
ahead of Manitoba. The river flat was dotted with clumps
of russet-leaved willows, to the north of which our waggons
were ranged, and soon the quickly pitched tents, fires and
sizzling fry-pans filled even the tenderfoot with a sense of
comfort.

Next morning our route lay through a line of low, broken
hills, with scattered woods, largely burnt and blown down
by the wind; a desolate tract, which enclosed, to our left,
the Lily Lake—Ascútamo Sakaigon—a somewhat marshy-

looking sheet of water. Some miles farther on we crossed
Whiskey Creek, a white man's name, of course, given by
an illicit distiller, who throve for a time, in the old " Permit
days," in this secluded spot. Beyond this the long line of
the Vermilion Hills hove in sight, and presently we reached
the Vermilion River, the Wyamun of the Crees, and, before
nightfall, the Nasookamow, or Twin Lake, making our camp
in an open besmirched pinery, a cattle shelter, with bleak
and bare surroundings, neighboured by the shack of a solitary settler. He had, no doubt, good reasons for his choice;
but it seemed a very much less inviting locality than Stony
Creek, which we came to next morning, approaching it
through rich and massive spruce woods, the ground strewn
with anemones, harebells and violets, and interspersed with
almost startlingly snow-white poplars, whose delicate buds
had just opened into leaf.

Stony Creek is a tributary of a larger stream, called the
Tawutináow, which means " a passage between hills." This
is an interesting spot, for here is the height of land, the
" divide " between the Saskatchewan and the Athabasca,
between Arctic and Hudson Bay waters, the stream before
us flowing north, and carrying the yellowish-red tinge common to the waters on this slope. A great valley to the left
of the trail runs parallel with it from the Sturgeon to the
Tawutináow, evidently the channel of an ancient river,
whose course it would now be difficult to determine without
close examination. At all events, it stretches almost from
the Saskatchewan to the Athabasca, and indicates some great
watershed in times past. Hay was abundant here, and
much stock, it was evident, might be raised in the district.

Towards evening we reached the Tawutináow bridge, some
eighteen miles from the Landing, our finest camp, dry and
pleasant, with sward and copse and a fine stream close by.
Here is an extensive peat bed, which was once on fire and
burnt for years—a great peril to freighters' ponies, which
sometimes grazed into its unseen but smouldering depths.

The seat of the fire was now an immense grassy circle, with a low wall of blackened peat all around it.

In the morning an endless succession of small creeks was passed, screened by deep valleys which fell in from hills and muskegs to the south, and at noon, jaded with slow travel, we reached Athabasca Landing. A long hill leads down to the flat, and from its brow we had a striking view of the village below and of the noble river, which much resembles the Saskatchewan, minus its prairies. We were now fairly within the bewildering forest of the north, which spreads, with some intervals of plain, to the 69th parallel of north latitude; an endless jungle of shaggy spruce, black and white poplar, birch, tamarack and Banksian pine. At the Landing we pitched our tents in front of the Hudson's Bay Company's post, where had stood, the previous year, a big canvas town of "Klondikers." Here they made preparation for their melancholy journey, setting out on the great stream in every species of craft, from rafts and coracles to steam barges. Here was begun an episode of that world-wide craze, which has run through all time, and almost every country, in which were enacted deeds of daring and suffering which add a new chapter to the history of human fearlessness and folly.

The Landing was a considerable hamlet for such a wilderness, being the shipping point to Mackenzie River, and, *via* the Lesser Slave Lake, to the Upper Peace. It consisted of the Hudson's Bay Company's establishment, with large storehouses, a sawmill, the residence and church of a Church of England bishop, and a Roman Catholic station, with a variety of shelters in the shape of boarding-houses, shacks and tepees all around. From the number of scows and barges in all stages of construction, and the high timber canting-tackles, it had quite a shipyard-like look, the population being mainly mechanics, who constructed scows, small barges, called "sturgeons," and the old "York," or inland boat, carrying from four to five tons. Here, hauled up on the bank, was the Hudson's Bay Company's steamer, the *Athabasca,* a well-built vessel about 160 feet long by 28 feet beam. This vessel, it was found, drew too much water for the channel; so there she lay, rotting upon her skids. It was a tantalizing sight to ourselves, who would have been spared many a heart-break had she been fit for service. A more interesting feature of the Landing, however, was the well sunk by the Government borer, Mr. Fraser, for oil, but which sent up gas instead. The latter was struck at a considerable depth, and, when we were there, was led from the shaft under the river bank by a pipe, from which it issued aflame, burning constantly, we were told, summer and winter. Standing at the gateway of the unknown North, and looking at this interesting feature, doubly so from its place and promise, one could not but forecast an industrial future, and "dream on things to come."

Shortly after our arrival at the Landing, news, true or false, reached us that the ice was still fast on Lesser Slave Lake. At any rate, the boat's crew expected from there did not turn up, and a couple of days were spent in anxious waiting. Some freight was delayed as well, and a thunder-storm and a night of rain set the camp in a swim. The non-arrival of our trackers was serious, as we had two scows and a York boat, with a party all told of some fifty souls, and only thirteen available trackers to start with. It seemed more than doubtful whether we could reach Lesser Slave Lake on treaty-schedule time, and the anxiety to push on was great. It was decided to set out as we were and trust to the chapter of accidents. We did not foresee the trials before us, the struggle up a great and swift river, with contrary winds, rainy weather, weak tracking lines and a weaker crew. The chapter of accidents opened, but not in the expected manner.

The York boat and one of the scows were fitted up amid-ships with an awning, which could be run down on all sides when required, but were otherwise open to the weather, and

3

much encumbered with lading; but all things being in readiness, on the 3rd of June we took to the water, and, a photograph of the scene having been taken, shoved off from the Landing. The boats were furnished with long, cumbrous sweeps, yet not a whit too heavy, since numbers of them snapped with the vigorous strokes of the rowers during the trip. A small sweep, passed through a ring at the stern, served as a rudder, by far the best steering gear for the "sturgeons," but not for a York boat, which is built with a keel and can sail pretty close to the wind. Ordinarily the only sail in use is a lug, which has a great spread, and moves a boat quickly in a fair wind. In a calm, of course, sweeps have to be used, and our first step in departure was to cross the river with them, the boatmen rising with the oars and falling back simultaneously to their seats with perfect precision, and handling the great blades with practised ease. When the opposite shore was reached, the four trackers of each boat leaped into the water, and, splashing up the bank, got into harness at once, and began, with changes to the oars, the unflagging pull which lasted for two weeks. This harness is called by the trackers "otapanápi" —a Cree word—and it must be borne in mind that scarcely any language was spoken throughout this region other than Cree. A little English or French was occasionally heard; but the tongue, domestic, diplomatic, universal, was Cree, into which every half-breed in common talk lapsed, sooner or later, with undisguised delight. It was his mother tongue, copious enough to express his every thought and emotion, and its soft accents, particularly in the mouth of woman, are certainly very musical. Emerson's phrase, "fossil poetry," might be applied to our Indian languages, in which a single stretched-out word does duty for a sentence.

But to the harness. This is simply an adjustment of leather breast-straps for each man, tied to a very long tracking line, which, in turn, is tied to the bow of the boat. The trackers, once in it, walk off smartly along the bank, the men on board keeping the boats clear of it, and, on a fair path, with good water, make very good time. Indeed, the pull seems to give an impetus to the trackers as well as to the boat, so that a loose man has to lope to keep up with them. But on bad paths and bad water the speed is sadly pulled down, and, if rapids occur, sinks to the zero of a few miles a day. The " spells " vary according to these circumstances, but half an hour is the ordinary pull between " pipes," and there being no shifts in our case, the stoppages for rest and tobacco were frequent. At this rate we calculated that it would take eight or ten days to reach the mouth of Lesser Slave River. Mr. d'Eschambault and myself, having experienced the crowded state of the first and second boats, and foregathered during the trip, decided to take up our quarters on the scow, which had no awning, but which offered some elbow room and a tolerably cozy nook amongst the cases, bales and baggage with which it was encumbered.

We had a study on board, as well, in our steersman, Pierre Cyr, which partly attracted me—a bronzed man, with long, thin, yet fine weather-beaten features, frosty moustache and keenly-gazing, dry, gray eyes—a tall, slim and sinewy man, over seventy years of age, yet agile and firm of step as a man of thirty. Add the semi-silent, inward laugh which Cooper ascribes to his Leather-Stocking, and you have Pierre Cyr, who might have stood for that immortal's portrait. That he had a history I felt sure when I first saw him seated amongst his boatmen at the Landing, and, on seeking his acquaintance, was not surprised to learn that he had accompanied Sir John Richardson on his last journey in Prince Rupert's Land, and Dr. Rae on his eventful expedition to Repulse Bay, in 1853, in search of Franklin. He looked as if he could do it again—a vigorous, alert man, ready and able to track or pole with the best—a survivor, in fact, of the old race of Red River voyageurs, whose record is one of the romances of history.

Another attraction was my companion, Mr. d'E. himself —a man stout in person, quiet by disposition, and of few words; a man, too, with a lineage which connected him with many of the oldest pioneer families of French Canada. His ancestor, Jacques Alexis d'Eschambault, originally of St. Jean de Montaign, in Poictou, came to New France in the 17th century, where, in 1667, he married Marguerite Rene Denys, a relative of the devoted Madame de la Peltrie, and thus became brother-in-law to M. de Ramezay, the owner of the famous old mansion in Montreal, now a museum. Jacques d'Eschambault's son married a daughter of Louis Joliet, the discoverer of the Mississippi, and became a prominent merchant in Quebec, distinguishing himself, it is said, by having the largest family ever known in Canada, viz., thirty-two children. Under the new *régime* my companion's grandfather, like many another French Canadian gentleman, entered the British army, but died in Canada, leaving as heir to his seigneurie a young man whose friendship for Lord Selkirk led him to Red River as a companion, where he subsequently entered the Hudson's Bay Company's service, and died, a chief-factor, at St. Boniface, Man. His son, my companion, also entered the service, in 1857, at his father's post of Isle a la Crosse, served seven years at Cumberland, nine at other distant points, and, finally, fifteen years as trader at Reindeer Lake, a far northern post bordering on the Barren Lands, and famous for its breed of dogs. My friend had some strange virtues, or defects, as the ungodly might call them; he had never used tobacco or intoxicants in his life, a marvellous thing considering his environment. He possessed, besides, a fine simplicity which pleased one. Doubled up in the Edmonton hotel with a waggish companion, he was seen, so the latter affirmed, to attempt to blow out the electric light, a thing which, greatly to his discomfiture, was done by his bed-fellow with apparent ease. Being a man of scant speech, I enjoyed with him betimes the luxury of it. But we had much discourse for all that, and I learnt many interesting things from this old trader, who seemed taciturn in our little crowd, but was, in reality, a tower of intelligent silence beat about by a flood of good-humoured chaff and loquacity.

At our first night's camp we were still in sight of the Landing, which looked absurdly near, considering the men's hard pull; and from there messengers were sent to Baptiste Lake, the source of Baptiste Creek, which joins the Athabasca a few miles up, and where there was a settlement of half-breed fishermen and hunters, to procure additional trackers if possible. On their unsuccessful return, at eleven a.m., we started again—newo pishawuk, as they call it, "four trackers to the line," as before—and early in the afternoon were opposite Baptiste Creek, and, weather compelling, rowed across, and camped there that evening. It rained dismally all night, and morning opened with a strong head wind and every symptom of bad weather. A survey party from the Rocky Mountains, in a York boat, tarried at our camp, bringing word that the ice-jam was clear in Lesser Slave Lake, which was cheering, but that we need scarcely look for the expected assistance. They also gave a vague account of the murder of a squaw by her husband for cannibalism, which afterwards proved to be groundless, and, with this comforting information, sped on.

It is ridiculously easy to go down the Athabasca compared with ascending it. The previous evening a Baptiste Lake hunter, bound for the Landing, set out from our camp at a great rate astride of a couple of logs, which he held together with his legs, and disappeared round the bend below in a twinkling. A priest, too, with a companion, arrived about dusk in a canoe, and set off again, intending to beach at the Landing before dark.

Of course, several surmises were current regarding the non-arrival of our trackers, the most likely being Bishop Grouard's, that, as the R. C. Mission boats and men had not come down either, the Indians and half-breeds were too intent upon discussing the forthcoming treaty to stir.

So far it had been the rain and consequent bad tracking which had delayed us; but still we were too weak-handed to make headway without help, and it was at this juncture that the Police contingent stepped manfully into the breach, and volunteered to track one of the boats to the lake. This was no light matter for men unaccustomed to such beastly toil and in such abominable weather; but, having once put their hands to the rope, they were not the men to back down. With unfaltering " go " they pulled on day after day, landing their boat at its destination at last, having worked in the harness and at the sweeps, without relief, from the start almost to the finish.

Meanwhile all enjoyed good health and spirits in spite of the weather. There were fair grounds for the belief that Mr. Ross, who had set out by trail from Edmonton, would reach the lake in time to distribute to the congregated Indians and half-breeds the Government rations stored there for that purpose, and, therefore, our anxiety was not so great as it would otherwise have been.

Our trackers being thus reinforced, the outlook was more satisfactory, not so much in increased speed as in the certainty of progress. The rain had ceased, and though the sky was still lowering, the temperature was higher. Tents were struck, and the boats got under way at once, taking chances on the weather, which, instead of breaking up in another deluge, improved. Eight men were now put to each line, Peokus, a remarkable old Blackfoot Indian, captured and adopted in boyhood by the Crees, and who afterwards attracted the attention of us all, being detailed to lead the Police gang, who, raw and unused to the work, required an experienced tracker at their head.

The country passed through hitherto was rolling, hilly, and densely forested, but, alas, with prostrate trunks and fire-blasted " rampikes," which ranged in all directions in desolate profusion. The timber was Banksian pine, spruce, poplar and birch, much of it merchantable, but not of large size. It was pitiful to see so much wealth destroyed by

recent fires, and that, too, at the possible opening of an era
of real value in the near future.   The greatest destruction
was evidently on the north side of the river, but the south
had not escaped.

As regards the soil in these parts, it was, so far, impossible to speak favourably.   The hunters described the inland
country as a wilderness of sand-hills, surrounded by quak-
ing-bogs, muskegs and soft meadows.   Judging by exposures
on the river bank, there are, here and there, fertile areas
which may yet be utilized; but probably the best thing that
could happen to that part of the country would be a great
clearing fire to complete the destruction of its dead timber
and convert its best parts into prairie and a summer range
for cattle.

We were now approaching a portion of the river where
the difficulties of getting on were great.   The men had to
cope with the swift current, bordered by a series of steep
gumbo slides, where the tracking was hazardous; where
great trees slanted over the water, tottering to their fall, or
deep pits and fissures gaped in the festering clay, into which
the men often plunged to their arm-pits.   It was horrible
to look upon.   The chain-gang, the galley-slaves—how often
the idea of them was recalled by that horrid pull!   Yet
onward they went, with teeth set and hands bruised by the
rope, surmounting difficulty after difficulty with the pith of
lions.

At last a better region was reached, with occasionally a
better path.   Here the destruction by fire had been stayed,
the country improved, and the forest outlines became bold
and noble.   Hour by hour we crept along a like succession
of majestic bends of the river, not yet flushed by the summer
freshet, but flowing with superb volume and force.   Fully
ten miles were made that day, the men tracking like Trojans
through water and over difficult ground, but fortunately free
from mosquitoes, the constant head winds keeping these
effectually down.   The cool weather in like manner kept the
water down, for it is in this month that the freshet from the

Rocky Mountains generally begins, filling the channel bank-high, submerging the tracking paths, and bearing upon its foaming surface such a mass of uprooted trees and river trash that it is almost impossible to make head against it.

The next morning opened dry and pleasant, but with a milky and foreboding sky. Again the boats were in motion, passing the Pusquatenáo, or Naked Hill, beyond which is the Echo Lake—Katoó Sakaígon—where a good many Indians lived, having a pack-trail thereto from the river.

The afternoon proved to be hot, the clouds cumulose against a clear, blue sky, with occasional sun-showers. The tracking became better for a time, the lofty benches decreasing in height as we ascended. Innumerable ice-cold creeks poured in from the forest, all of a reddish-yellow cast, and the frequent marks on trees, informing passing hunters of the success of their friends, and the number of stages along the shore for drying meat, indicated a fine moose country.

The next day was treaty day, and we were still a long way from the treaty post. The Police, not yet hardened to the work, felt fagged, but would not own up, a nephew of Sir William Vernon Harcourt bringing up the rear, and all slithering, but hanging to it with dogged perseverance. Nothing, indeed, can be imagined more arduous than this tracking up a swift river, against constant head winds in bad weather. Much of it is in the water, wading up " snies," or tortuous shallow channels, plunging into numberless creeks, clambering up slimy banks, creeping under or passing the line over fallen trees, wading out in the stream to round long spits of sand or boulders, floundering in gumbo slides, tripping, crawling, plunging, and, finally, tottering to the camping-place sweating like horses, and mud to the eyes—but never grumbling. After a whole day of this slavish work, no sooner was the bath taken, supper stowed, and pipes filled, than laughter began, and jokes and merriment ran round the camp-fires as if such things as mud and toil had never existed.

An awkward spot

Severe tracking up the Athabasca River

On the rocks

The old Indian, Peokus, heading the Police line, was a study. His garb was a pair of pants toned down to the colour of the grime they daily sank in, a shirt and corduroy vest to match, a faded kerchief tied around his head, an Assomption sash, and a begrimed body inside of all—a short, squarely built frame, clad with rounded muscles— nothing angular about *him!*—but the nerves within tireless as the stream he pulled against. On the lead, in harness, his long arms swung like pendulums, his whole body leant forward at an acute angle, the gait steady, and the step solid as the tramp of a gorilla. Some coarse black hairs clung here and there to his upper lip; his fine brown eyes were embedded in wrinkles, and his swarthy features, though clumsy, were kindly—a good-humoured face, which, at a cheerful word or glance, lit up at once with the grotesque grin of an animated gargoyle. This was the typical old-time tracker of the North; the toiler who brought in the pro- ducts of man's art in the East, and took out Nature's returns —the Indian's output—ever since the trade first penetrated these endless solitudes.

The forest scenery now became very striking; primeval masses of poplar and birch foliage, which spread away and upward in smoothest slopes, like vast lawns, studded with the sombre green of the pine tops which towered above them. Here and there the bends of the river crossed at such angles as to enclose a lake-like expanse of water. The river also took a fine colouring from its tributaries, a sort of greenish- yellow tinge, and now became flecked with bubbles and thin foam, so that we feared the freshet, which would have been disastrous.

At mid-day we reached Shoal Island—Pakwáo Ministic— and here the poles were got out and the trackers took the middle of the river for nearly a mile, until deep water was reached. Placer miners had evidently been at work here, but with poor results, we were told. Below Baptiste Creek, however, the yield had been satisfactory, and several miners had made from $2.00 to $2.50 a day over their living expenses. Above the Baptiste there was nothing doing; indeed, we did not pass a single miner at work on the whole route, and it was the best time for their work. The gold is flocculent, its source as mysterious as that of the Saskatchewan, if the theory that the latter was washed out of the Selkirks before the upheaval of the Rockies is astray.

A fresh moose head, seen lying on the bank, indicated a hunting party, but no human life was seen aside from our own people. Indeed, the absence of life of any kind along the river, excepting the song-birds, which were in some places numerous, was surprising. No deer, no bears, not even a fox or a timber wolf made one's fingers itch for the trigger. A few brent, which took wing afar off, and a high-flying duck or two, were the sole wildings observed, save a big humble-bee which droned around our boat for an instant, then darted off again. Even fish seemed to be anything but plentiful.

That night's camp was hurriedly made in a hummocky fastness of pine and birch, where we found few comfortable bedding-places. In the morning we passed several ice-ledges along shore, the survivals of the severe winter, and, presently, met a canoe with two men from Peace River, crest-fallen " Klondikers," who had " struck it rich," they said, with a laugh, and who reported good water. Next morning a very early start was made, and after some long, strong pulls, and a vigorous spurt, the mouth of the Lesser Slave River opened at last on our sight.

We had latterly passed along what appeared to be fertile soil, a sandy clay country, which improved to the west and south-west at every turn. It had an inviting look, and the " lie," as well, of a region foreordained for settlement. It was irritating not to be able to explore the inner land, but our urgency was too great for that. From what we saw, however, it was easy to predict that thither would flow, in time, the stream of pioneer life and the bustle of attending enterprise and trade.

CHAPTER II.

LESSER SLAVE RIVER AND LESSER SLAVE LAKE.

IT is unnecessary to inform the average reader that the Lesser Slave River connects the Lesser Slave Lake with the Athabasca; any atlas will satisfy him upon that point. But its peculiar colouring he will not find there, and it is this which gives the river its most distinctive character. Once seen, it is easy to account for the hue of the Athabasca below the Lesser Slave River; for the water of the latter, though of a pale yellow colour in a glass, is of a rich burnt umber in the stream, and when blown upon by the wind turns its sparkling facets to the sun like the smile upon the cheek of a brunette. Its upward course is like a continuous letter S with occasional S's side by side, so that a point can be crossed on foot in a few minutes which would cost much time to go around. Its proper name, too, is not to be found in the atlases, either English or French. There it is called the Lesser Slave River, but in the classic Cree its name is Iyaghchi Eennu Sepe, or the River of the Blackfeet, literally the " River of the Strange People." The lake itself bears the same name, and even now is never called Slave Lake by the Indians in their own tongue. This fact, to my mind, casts additional light upon an obscure prehistoric question, namely, the migration of the great Algic, or Algonquin, race. Its early home was, perhaps, in the far south, or south-west, whence it migrated around the Gulf of Florida, and eastward along the Atlantic coast, spreading up its bays and inlets, and along its great tributary rivers, finally penetrating by the Upper Ottawa to James's, and ultimately to the shores of

Hudson Bay. I know there is strong adverse opinion as to the starting-point of this migration, and I only offer my own as a suggestion based upon the facts stated, and as, therefore, worthy of consideration. Sir Alexander Mackenzie speaks of the Blackfeet " travelling north-westward," and that the Crees were " invaders of the Saskatchewan from the eastward." Indeed, he says the latter were called by the Hudson's Bay Company's officers at York Factory " their home-guards." One thing seems certain, viz., that the Crees got their fire-arms from the English at Hudson Bay in the 17th century. Thence that great tribe, called by themselves the Nahéowuk, but by the Ojibway Saulteaux the Kinistineaux, and by the voyageurs Christineaux, or, more commonly, the Crees—a word derived, some think, from the first syllable of the latter name, or perhaps from the French *crier,* to shout— descended upon the Blackfeet, who probably at that time occupied this region, and undoubtedly the Saskatchewan, and drove them south along a line stretching to the Rocky Mountains.

The tradition of this expulsion is still extant, as also of the great raids made by the Blackfeet and their kindred in times past into their ancient domain. I remember visiting, with my old friend Attakacoop—Star-Blanket—the deceased Cree chief, twenty years ago, the triumphal pile of red deer horns raised by the Blackfeet north of Shell River, a tributary of the North Saskatchewan. It is called by the Crees Ooskunaka Assustakee, and the chief described its great size in former days, and the tradition of its origin as told to him in his boyhood. Be all this as it may, and this is not the place to pursue the inquiry, the stream in question is, to the Crees who live upon it, not the River of the Slaves, but the " River of the Blackfeet." How it came by its white name is another question. Possibly some captured Indians of the tribe called the Slaves to this day, reduced to servitude by the Crees, were seen by the early voyageurs, and gave rise to the French name, of which ours is a translation.

Slavery was common enough amongst the Indians everywhere. A thriving trade was done at the Detroit in the
18th century in Pawnees, or Panis, as they were called, captured by Indian raiders on the western prairies and sold to
the white settlers along the river. I have seen in Windsor,
Ont., an old bill of sale of one of these Pani slaves, the consideration being, if I recollect aright, a certain quantity of
Indian corn.

To return to the river. The distance from Athabasca
Landing to the Lesser Slave is called sixty-five miles, but
this must have been ascertained by measuring from point to
point, for, following the shore up stream, as boats must, it
is certainly more. To the head of the river is an additional
sixty miles, and thence to the head of the lake seventy-five
more. The Hudson's Bay Company had a storehouse at the
Forks, and an island was forming where the waters meet,
the finest feature of the place being an echo, which reverber-
ated the bugler's call at *reveille* very grandly.

A spurt was made in the early morning, the trackers first
following a bank overgrown with alders and sallows, all of
a size, which looked exactly like a well-kept hedge, but soon
gave way to the usual dense line of poplar and spruce, rooted
to the very edges of the banks, which are low compared with
those of the Athabasca. After ascending it for some distance, it being Sunday, we camped for the day upon an open
grassy point, around which the river swept in a perfect semi-
circle, the dense forest opposite towering in one equally perfect, and glorious in light and shade and harmonious tints of
green, from sombre olive to the lightest pea. The point
itself was covered with strawberry vines and dotted with
clumps of saskatoons all in bloom.

It was a lovely and lonely spot, which was soon converted
into a scene of eating and laughter, and a drying ground for
wet clothes. Towards evening Bishop Grouard and Father
Lacombe held a well-attended service, which in this profound
wilderness was peculiarly impressive. Listening, one thought

how often the same service, these same chants and canticles, had awakened the sylvan echoes in like solitudes on the St. Lawrence and Mississippi in the old days of exploration and trade, and of missionary zeal and suffering. It recalled, too, the thought of man's evanescence and the apparent fixedness of his institutions.

Shortly after our tents were pitched a boat drifted past with five jaded-looking men aboard—more baffled Klondikers returning from Peace River. We had heard of numbers in the interior who could neither go on nor return, and expected to meet more castaways before we reached the lake. In this we were not astray, and several days after in the upper river we met a York boat loaded with them—alert and unmistakable Americans, but with the worn features of disappointed men.

We were now constantly encountering the rapids, which extended for about twenty-five miles, and very difficult and troublesome they proved to be to our heavily-loaded craft. Most of them were got over slowly by combined poling and tracking, the line often breaking with the strain, and the boats being kept in the channel only by the most strenuous efforts of the experienced men on board. If a monias (a greenhorn) took the bow pole, as was sometimes the case, the orders of our steersman, Cyr, were amusing to listen to. "Tughkenay asswayegh tamook!" (Be on your guard!) "Turn de oder way! Turn yourself! Turn your pole—*Hell!*" Then, of course, came the customary rasp on the rocks, but, if not, the cheery cry followed to the trackers ashore, "Ahchipitamook!" (Haul away!) and on we would go for a few yards more. Once, towards the end of this dreary business, when we were all crowded into the Commissioner's boat, where we took our meals, in the first really stiff rapid the keel grated as usual upon the rocks. With a better line we might have pulled through, but it broke, and the boat at once swung broadside to the current and listed on the rocks immovably, though the men struggling in the water did their best to heave her off. The third boat then came up, and

shortly afterwards the Police boat.   But getting their steering sweeps fouled and lines entangled, it was nearly an hour
before Cyr's boat, being first lightened, could swing to star-
board of the York, and take off the passengers.   The York
boat was then shouldered off the rocks by main force, and all
got under way again.   At this juncture our old Indian,
Peokus—or Pehayokusk, to give him his right name, to wit,
" The giblets of a bird "—met with a serious accident, which,
much to our regret, laid him up for several days.   In his
eagerness to help he slipped from a sunken log, and the
bruise knocked the wind out of him completely.   We took off
his wet clothes and rubbed him, and laid him by the fire,
where the doctor's care and a liberal dram of spirits soon
fetched him to rights.   A look of pleased wonder passed over
his clumsy features as the latter did its work.   Caliban himself could not have been more curiously surprised.

This was not our last stick: there were other awkward
rapids near by; but by dint of wading, shouldering, pulling
and tracking, we got over the last of them and into a deep
channel for good, having advanced only five miles after a
day of incessant toil, most of it in the water.

Our camp that night was a memorable one.   The day was
the fiftieth anniversary of Father Lacombe's ministration
as a missionary in the North-West, and all joined in presenting him with a suitable address, handsomely engrossed
by Mr. Prudhomme on birch bark, and signed by the whole
party.   A poem, too, composed by Mr. Coté, a gentleman
of literary gifts and taste, also written on bark, was read
and presented at the same time.*   Père Lacombe made a
touching impromptu reply, which was greatly appreciated.
Many of us were not of the worthy Father's communion, yet
there was but one feeling, that of deep respect for the labours
of this celebrated missionary, whose life had been a continuous effort to help the unbefriended Indian into the new but

---

* The poem, the text of which was secured from the author too late for
insertion here, will be found in the Appendix, p. 490.

inevitable paths of self-support, and to shield him from the rapacity of the cold incoming world now surging around him. After the presentation, over a good cigar, the Father told some inimitable stories of Indian life on the plains in the old days, which to my great regret are too lengthy for inclusion here. One incident, however, being *apropos* of himself, must find place. Turning the conversation from materialism, idealism, and the other "isms" into which it had drifted, he spoke of the fears so many have of ghosts, and even of a corpse, and confessed that, from early training, he had shared this fear until he got rid of it in an incident one winter at Lac Ste. Anne. He had been sent for during the night to administer extreme unction to a dying half-breed girl thirteen miles away. Hitching his dogs to their sled he sped on, but too late, for he was met on the trail by the girl's relatives, bringing her dead body wrapped in a buffalo skin, and which they asked him to take back with him and place in his chapel pending service. He tremblingly assented, and the body was duly tied to his sled, the relatives returning to their homes. He was alone with the corpse in the dense and dark forest, and felt the old dread, but reflecting on his office and its duties, he ran for a long distance behind the sled until, thoroughly tired, he stepped on it to rest. In doing this he slipped and fell upon the corpse in a spasm of fear, which, strange to say, when he recovered from it, he felt no more. The shock cured him, and, reaching home, he placed the girl's body in the chapel with his own hands. It reminded him, he said, of a Community at Marseilles whose Superior had died, but whose money was missing. The new Superior sent a young priest who had a great dread of ghosts down to the crypt below the church to open the coffin and search the pockets of the dead. He did so, and found the money; but in nailing on the coffin lid again, a part of his soutane was fastened down with it. The priest turned to go, advanced a step, and, being suddenly held, dropped dead with fright. These gruesome stories were happily followed by an hour or two of song and pleasantry in Mr. McKenna's tent, ending in " Auld Lang Syne " and " God Save the Queen." It was a unique occasion in which to wind up so laborious a day; and our camp itself was unique—on a lofty bluff overlooking the confluence of the Saulteau River with the Lesser Slave—a bold and beautiful spot, the woods at the angle of the two rivers, down to the water's edge, showing like a gigantic V, as clean-cut as if done by a pair of colossal shears.

Next morning rowing took the place of poling and tracking for a time, and, presently, the great range of lofty hills called, to our right, the Moose Watchi, and to our left, the Tuskanatchi—the Moose and Raspberry Mountains—loomed in the distance. Here, and when only a few miles from the lake, a York boat came tearing down stream full of lithe, young half-breed trackers—our long-expected assistants from the Hudson's Bay Company's post, and whom we would have welcomed much more warmly had they come sooner, for we had little but the lake now to ascend, up which a fair breeze would carry us in a single night.

Doubtless it would have done so if it had come; but the same head-winds and storms which had thwarted us from the first dogged us still. We had camped near the mouth of Muskeg Creek, a good-sized stream, and evidently the cause hitherto of the Lesser Slave's rich chocolate colour; for, above the forks, the latter took its hue from the lake, but with a yellowish tinge still. From this point the river was very crooked, and lined by great hay meadows of luxuriant growth. Skirting these, reinforced as we were, we soon pulled up to the foot of the lake, where stood a Hudson's Bay Company's solitary storehouse. There some change of lading was made, in order to reach " the Island," some seven miles up, and the only one in the lake, sails being hoisted for the first time to an almost imperceptible wind.

The island, where we were to camp simply for the night— as we fondly thought—was found to be a sprawling jumble

4

of water-worn pebbles, boulders and sand, with a long narrow spit projecting to the east, much frequented by gulls, of whose eggs a large number were gathered. To the south, on the mainland, is the site of the old North-West Company's post, near to which stood that of the Hudson's Bay Company, for they always planted themselves cheek by jowl in those days of rivalry, so that there should be no lack of provocation. A dozen half-breed families had now their habitat there, and subsisted by fishing and trapping. On the island our Cree half-breeds enjoyed the first evening's camp by playing the universal button-hiding game called Pugas̃-awin, and which is always accompanied by a monotonous chant and the tom-tom, anything serving for that hideous instrument if a drum is not at hand. They are all inveterate gamblers in that country, and lose or win with equal indifference. Others played a peculiar game of cards called Natwawáquawin, or "Marriage," the loser's penalty being droll, but unmentionable. These amusements, which often spun out till morning, were broken up by another rattling storm, which lasted all night and all the next day. We had lost all count of storms by this time, and were stolidly resigned. The day following, however, the wind was fresh and fair, and we made great headway, reaching the mouth of Swan River—Naposéo Sepe—about mid-day.

This stream is almost choked at its discharge by a conglomeration of slimy roots, weeds and floatwood, and the banks are "a melancholy waste of putrid marshes." It is a forbidding entrance to a river which, farther up, waters a good farming country, including coal in abundance.

The wind being strong and fair, we spun along at a great rate, and expected to reach the treaty point before dark, reckoning, as usual, without our host. The wind suddenly wheeled to the south-west, and a dangerous squall sprang up, which forced us to run back for shelter fully five miles. There was barely time to camp before the gale became furious, raging all night, and throwing down tents like nine-

pins. About one a.m. a cry arose from the night-watch that
the boats were swamping. All hands turned out, lading was
removed, and the scows hauled up on the shingle, the rollers
piling on shore with a height and fury perfectly astonishing
for such a lake. By morning the tempest was at its height,
continuing all day and into the night. The sunset that evening exhibited some of the grandest and wildest sky scenery
we had ever beheld. In the west a vast bank of luminous
orange cloud, edged by torn fringes of green and gray; in
the south a sea of amethyst, and stretching from north to
east masses of steel gray and pearl, shot with brilliant shafts
and tufts of golden vapour. The whole sky streamed with
rich colouring in the fierce wind, as if possessed at once by
the genii of beauty and storm. The boatmen, noting its
aspect, predicted worse weather; but, fortunately, morning
belied the omens—our trials were over.

We were now nearing Shaw's Point, a long willowed spit
of land, called after a whimsical old chief-factor of the Hudson's Bay Company who had charge of this district over sixty
years before. He appears to have been a man of many eccen-
tricities, one of which was the cultivation *a la Chinois* of a
very long finger-nail, which he used as a spoon to eat his
egg. But of him anon. By four p.m. we had rounded his
Point, and come into view of Wyaweekamon—" The Outlet "—a rudimentary street with several trading stores, a
billiard saloon and other accessories of a brand-new village in
a very old wilderness.

Here we were at the treaty point at last, safe and sound,
with new interests and excitements before us; with wild man
instead of wild weather to encounter; with discords to harmonize and suspicions to allay by human kindness, perhaps by
human firmness, but mainly by the just and generous terms
proffered by Government to an isolated but highly interesting
and deserving people.

CHAPTER III.

TREATY AT LESSER SLAVE LAKE.

On the 19th of June our little fleet landed at Willow Point. There was a rude jetty, or wharf, at this place, below the little trading village referred to, at which loaded boats discharged. Formerly they could ascend the sluggish and shallow channel connecting the expansion of the Heart River, called Buffalo Lake, with the head of Lesser Slave Lake, a distance of about three miles, and as far as the Hudson's Bay Company's post, around which another trading village had gathered. This temporary fall in the water level partly accounted for the growth of the village at Willow Point, where sufficient interests had arisen to cause a jealousy between the two hamlets. Once upon a time Atawaywé Kamick was supreme. This is the name the Crees give to the Hudson's Bay Company, meaning literally "the Buying House." But now there were many stores, and "free trade" was rather in the ascendant. In the middle was safety, and therefore the Commissioners decided to pitch camp on a beautiful flat facing the south and fronting the channel, and midway between the two opposing points of trade. A *feu de joie* by the white residents of the region, of whom there were some seventy or eighty, welcomed the arrival of the boats at the wharf, and after a short stay here, simply to collect baggage, a start was made for the camping ground, where our numerous tents soon gave the place the appearance of a village of our own.

Tepees were to be seen in all directions from our camp—the lodges of the Indians and half-breeds. But no sooner was the treaty site apparent than a general concentration

52

Treaty Camp at Lesser Slave Lake

Indian Tepees

took place, and we were speedily surrounded by a bustling crowd, putting up trading tents and shacks, dancing booths, eating-places, etc., so that with the motley crowd, including a large number of women and children, and a swarm of dogs such as we never dreamt of, amounting in a short space by constant accessions to over a thousand, we were in the heart of life and movement and noise.

Mr. Ross, as already stated, had gone on by trail from Edmonton, partly in order to inspect it, and managed to reach the lake before us, which was fortunate, since Indians and half-breeds had collected in large numbers, and he was thus able to allay their irritation and to distribute rations pending the arrival of the other members of the Commission. During the previous winter, upon the circulation in the North of the news of the coming treaty, discussion was rife, and every cabin and tepee rang with argument. The wiseacre was not absent, of course, and agitators had been at work for some time endeavouring to jaundice the minds of the people —half-breeds, it was said, from Edmonton, who had been vitiated by contact with a low class of white men there—and, therefore, nothing was as yet positively known as to the temper and views of the Indians. But whatever evil effect these tamperings might have had upon them, it was felt that a plain statement of the proposals of the Government would speedily dissipate it, and that, when placed before them in Mr. Laird's customary kind and lucid manner, they would be accepted by both Indians and half-breeds as the best obtainable, and as conducing in all respects to their truest and most permanent interests.

On the 20th the eventful morning had come, and, for a wonder, the weather proved to be calm, clear and pleasant. The hour fixed upon for the beginning of negotiations was two p.m., up to which time much hand-shaking had, of course, to be undergone with the constant new arrivals of natives from the forest and lakes around. The Church of England and Roman Catholic clergy, the only missionary bodies in the country, met and dined with our party, after which all adjourned to the treaty ground, where the people had already assembled, and where all soon seated themselves on the grass in front of the treaty tent—a large marquee— the Indians being separated by a small space from the half-breeds, who ranged themselves behind them, all conducting themselves in the most sedate and orderly manner.

Mr. Laird and the other Commissioners were seated along the open front of the tent, and one could not but be impressed by the scene, set as it was in a most beautiful environment of distant mountains, waters, forests and meadows, all sweet and primeval, and almost untouched by civilized man. The whites of the region had also turned out to witness the scene, which, though lacking the wild aspect of the old assemblages on the plains in the early 'seventies, had yet a character of its own of great interest, and of the most hopeful promise.

The crowd of Indians ranged before the marquee had lost all semblance of wildness of the true type. Wild men they were, in a sense, living as they did in the forest and on their great waters. But it was plain that these people had achieved, without any treaty at all, a stage of civilization distinctly in advance of many of our treaty Indians to the south after twenty-five years of education. Instead of paint and feathers, the scalp-lock, the breech-clout, and the buffalo-robe, there presented itself a body of respectable-looking men, as well dressed and evidently quite as independent in their feelings as any like number of average pioneers in the East. Indeed, I had seen there, in my youth, many a time, crowds of white settlers inferior to these in sedateness and self-pos-session. One was prepared, in this wild region of forest, to behold some savage types of men; indeed, I craved to renew the vanished scenes of old. But, alas! one beheld, instead, men with well-washed, unpainted faces, and combed and common hair; men in suits of ordinary " store--clothes," and some even with " boiled " if not laundered shirts. One felt disappointed, almost defrauded. It was not what was expected, what we believed we had a right to expect, after so much waggoning and tracking and drenching, and river turmoil and trouble. This woeful shortcoming from bygone days attended other aspects of the scene. Instead of fiery oratory and pipes of peace—the stone calumets of old—the vigorous arguments, the outbursts of passion, and close calls from threatened violence, here was a gathering of commonplace men smoking briar-roots, with treaty tobacco instead of " weed," and whose chiefs replied to Mr. Laird's explanations and offers in a few brief and sensible statements, varied by vigorous appeals to the common sense and judgment, rather than the passions, of their people. It was a disappointing, yet, looked at aright, a gratifying spectacle. Here were men disciplined by good handling and native force out of barbarism—of which there was little to be seen—and plainly on the high road to comfort; men who led inoffensive and honest lives, yet who expressed their sense of freedom and self-support in their speech, and had in their courteous demeanour the unmistakable air and bearing of independence. If provoked by injustice, a very dangerous people this; but self-respecting, diligent and prosperous in their own primitive calling, and able to adopt agriculture, or any other pursuit, with a fair hope of success when the still distant hour for it should arrive.

The proceedings began with the customary distribution of tobacco, and by a reference to the competent interpreters who had been appointed by the Commission, men who were residents, and well known to the Indians themselves, and who possessed their confidence. The Indians had previously appointed as spokesman their Chief and head-man, Keenooshayoo and Moostoos, a worthy pair of brothers, who speedily exhibited their qualities of good sense and judgment, and, Keenooshayo in particular, a fine order of Indian eloquence, which was addressed almost entirely to his own people, and which is lost, I am sorry to say, in the account here set down.

Mr. Laird then rose, and having unrolled his Commission, and that of his colleagues, from the Queen, proceeded with his proposals. He spoke as follows:

"Red Brothers! we have come here to-day, sent by the Great Mother to treat with you, and this is the paper she has given to us, and is her Commission to us signed with her Seal, to show we have authority to treat with you. The other Commissioners, who are associated with me, and who are sitting here, are Mr. McKenna and Mr. Ross and the Rev. Father Lacombe, who is with us to act as counsellor and adviser. I have to say, on behalf of the Queen and the Government of Canada, that we have come to make you an offer. We have made treaties in former years with all the Indians of the prairie, and from there to Lake Superior. As white people are coming into your country, we have thought it well to tell you what is required of you. The Queen wants all the whites, half-breeds and Indians to be at peace with one another, and to shake hands when they meet. The Queen's laws must be obeyed all over the country, both by the whites and the Indians. It is not alone that we wish to prevent Indians from molesting the whites, it is also to prevent the whites from molesting or doing harm to the Indians. The Queen's soldiers are just as much for the protection of the Indians as for the white man. The Commissioners made an appointment to meet you at a certain time, but on account of bad weather on river and lake, we are late, which we are sorry for, but are glad to meet so many of you here to-day.

"We understand stories have been told you, that if you made a treaty with us you would become servants and slaves; but we wish you to understand that such is not the case, but that you will be just as free after signing a treaty as you are now. The treaty is a free offer; take it or not, just as you please. If you refuse it there is no harm done; we will not be bad friends on that account. One thing Indians must understand, that if they do not make a treaty they must

obey the laws of the land—that will be just the same whether
you make a treaty or not; the laws must be obeyed. The
Queen's Government wishes to give the Indians here the
same terms as it has given all the Indians all over the country, from the prairies to Lake Superior. Indians in other
places, who took treaty years ago, are now better off than
they were before. They grow grain and raise cattle like
the white people. Their children have learned to read and
write.

"Now, I will give you an outline of the terms we offer
you. If you agree to take treaty, every one this year gets
a present of $12.00. A family of five, man, wife and three
children, will thus get $60.00; a family of eight, $96.00;
and after this year, and for every year afterwards, $5.00
for each person forever. To such chiefs as you may select,
and that the Government approves of, we will give $25.00
each year, and the counsellors $15.00 each. The chiefs also
get a silver medal and a flag, such as you see now at our
tent, right now as soon as the treaty is signed. Next year,
as soon as we know how many chiefs there are, and every
three years thereafter, each chief will get a suit of clothes,
and every counsellor a suit, only not quite so good as that of
the chief. Then, as the white men are coming in and set-
tling in the country, and as the Queen wishes the Indians
to have lands of their own, we will give one square mile, or
640 acres, to each family of five; but there will be no com-
pulsion to force Indians to go into a reserve. He who does
not wish to go into a band can get 160 acres of land for
himself, and the same for each member of his family. These
reserves are holdings you can select when you please, subject to the approval of the Government, for you might select
lands which might interfere with the rights or lands of
settlers. The Government must be sure that the land which
you select is in the right place. Then, again, as some of you
may want to sow grain or potatoes, the Government will
give you ploughs or harrows, hoes, etc., to enable you to do

so, and every spring will furnish you with provisions to enable you to work and put in your crop. Again, if you do not wish to grow grain, but want to raise cattle, the Government will give you bulls and cows, so that you may raise stock. If you do not wish to grow grain or raise cattle, the Government will furnish you with ammunition for your hunt, and with twine to catch fish. The Government will also provide schools to teach your children to read and write, and do other things like white men and their children. Schools will be established where there is a sufficient number of children. The Government will give the chiefs axes and tools to make houses to live in and be comfortable. Indians have been told that if they make a treaty they will not be allowed to hunt and fish as they do now. This is not true. Indians who take treaty will be just as free to hunt and fish all over as they now are.

"In return for this the Government expects that the Indians will not interfere with or molest any miner, traveller or settler. We expect you to be good friends with every-one, and shake hands with all you meet. If any whites molest you in any way, shoot your dogs or horses, or do you any harm, you have only to report the matter to the police, and they will see that justice is done to you. There may be some things we have not mentioned, but these can be mentioned later on. Commissioners Walker and Coté are here for the half-breeds, who later on, if treaty is made with you, will take down the names of half-breeds and their children, and find out if they are entitled to scrip. The reason the Government does this is because the half-breeds have Indian blood in their veins, and have claims on that account. The Government does not make treaty with them, as they live as white men do, so it gives them scrip to settle their claims at once and forever. Half-breeds living like Indians have the chance to take the treaty instead, if they wish to do so. They have their choice, but only after the treaty is signed. If there is no treaty made, scrip cannot be given. After the treaty is signed, the Commissioners will take up half-breed claims.   The first thing they will do is to give half-breed settlers living on land 160 acres, if there is room to do so; but if several are settled close together, the land will be divided between them as fairly as possible.   All, whether settled or not, will be given scrip for land to the value of $240.00, that is, all born up to the date of signing the treaty. They can sell that scrip, that is, all of you can do so.   They can take, if they like, instead of this scrip for 240 acres, lands where they like.   After they have located their land, and got their title, they can live on it, or sell part, or the whole of it, as they please, but cannot sell the scrip.   They must locate their land, and get their title before selling.⁾

"These are the principal points in the offer we have to make to you.   The Queen owns the country, but is willing to acknowledge the Indians' claims, and offers them terms as an offset to all of them.   We shall be glad to answer any questions, and make clear any points not understood.   We shall meet you again to-morrow, after you have considered our offer, say about two o'clock, or later if you wish.   We have other Indians to meet at other places, but we do not wish to hurry you.   After this meeting you can go to the Hudson's Bay fort, where our provisions are stored, and rations will be issued to you of flour, bacon, tea and tobacco, so that you can have a good meal and a good time.   This is a free gift, given with goodwill, and given to you whether you make a treaty or not.   It is a present the Queen is glad to make to you.   I am now done, and shall be glad to hear what any one has to say."

KEENOOSHAYO (The Fish): "You say we are brothers. I cannot understand how we are so.   I live differently from you.   I can only understand that Indians will benefit in a very small degree from your offer.   You have told us you come in the Queen's name.   We surely have also a right to say a little as far as that goes.   I do not understand what you say about every third year."

Mr. McKenna: " The third year was only mentioned in connection with clothing."

Keenooshayo: " Do you not allow the Indians to make their own conditions, so that they may benefit as much as possible? Why I say this is that we to-day make arrangements that are to last as long as the sun shines and the water runs. Up to the present I have earned my own living and worked in my own way for the Queen. It is good. The Indian loves his way of living and his free life. When I understand you thoroughly I will know better what I shall do. Up to the present I have never seen the time when I could not work for the Queen, and also make my own living. I will consider carefully what you have said."

Moostoos (The Bull): " Often before now I have said I would carefully consider what you might say. You have called us brothers. Truly I am the younger, you the elder brother. Being the younger, if the younger ask the elder for something, he will grant his request the same as our mother the Queen. I am glad to hear what you have to say. Our country is getting broken up. I see the white man coming in, and I want to be friends. I see what he does, but it is best that we should be friends. I will not speak any more. There are many people here who may wish to speak."

Wahpeehayo (White Partridge): " I stand behind this man's back " (pointing to Keenooshayo). " I want to tell the Commissioners there are two ways, the long and the short. I want to take the way that will last longest."

Neesnetasis (The Twin): " I follow these two brothers, Moostoos and Keenooshayo. When I understand better I shall be able to say more."

Mr. Laird: " We shall be glad to hear from some of the Sturgeon Lake people."

The Captain (an old man): " I accept your offer. I am old and miserable now. I have not my family with me here, but I accept your offer."

Keenooshayo addressing the Commission at Lesser Slave Lake

Mr. Laird: " You will get the money for all your children under age, and not married, just the same as if they were here."

The Captain: " I speak for all those in my part of the country."

Mr. Laird: " I am sorry the rest of your people are not here. If here next year their claims will not be overlooked."

The Captain: " I am old now. It is indirectly through the Queen that we have lived. She has supplied in a manner the sale shops through which we have lived. Others may think I am foolish for speaking as I do now. Let them think as they like. I accept. When I was young I was an able man and made my living independently. But now I am old and feeble and not able to do much."

Mr. Ross: " I will just answer a few questions that have been put. Keenooshayo has said that he cannot see how it will benefit you to take treaty. As all the rights you now have will not be interfered with, therefore anything you get in addition must be a clear gain. The white man is bound to come in and open up the country, and we come before him to explain the relations that must exist between you, and thus prevent any trouble. You say you have heard what the Commissioners have said, and how you wish to live. We believe that men who have lived without help heretofore can do it better when the country is opened up. Any fur they catch is worth more. That comes about from competition. You will notice that it takes more boats to bring in goods to buy your furs than it did formerly. We think that as the rivers and lakes of this country will be the principal highways, good boatmen, like yourselves, cannot fail to make a good living, and profit from the increase in traffic. We are much pleased that you have some cattle. It will be the duty of the Commissioners to recommend the Government, through the Superintendent-General of Indian Affairs, to give you cattle of a better breed. You say that you consider that you have a right to say something about the terms we offer you. We offer you certain terms, but you are not forced to take them. You ask if Indians are not allowed to make a bargain. You must understand there are always two to a bargain. We are glad you understand the treaty is forever. If the Indians do as they are asked we shall certainly keep all our promises. We are glad to know that you have got on without any one's help, but you must know times are hard, and furs scarcer than they used to be. Indians are fond of a free life, and we do not wish to interfere with it. When reserves are offered you there is no intention to make you live on them if you do not want to, but, in years to come, you may change your minds, and want these lands to live on. The half-breeds of Athabasca are being more liberally dealt with than in any other part of Canada. We hope you will discuss our offer and arrive at a decision as soon as possible. Others are now waiting for our arrival, and you, by deciding quickly, will assist us to get to them."

KEENOOSHAYO: " Have you all heard? Do you wish to accept? All who wish to accept, stand up!"

WENDIGO: " I have heard, and accept with a glad heart all I have heard."

KEENOOSHAYO: " Are the terms good forever? As long as the sun shines on us? Because there are orphans we must consider, so that there will be nothing to be thrown up to us by our people afterwards. We want a written treaty, one copy to be given to us, so we shall know what we sign for. Are you willing to give means to instruct children as long as the sun shines and water runs, so that our children will grow up ever increasing in knowledge?"

MR. LAIRD: " The Government will choose teachers according to the religion of the band. If the band are pagans the Government will appoint teachers who, if not acceptable, will be replaced by others. About treaties lasting forever, I will just say that some Indians have got to live so like the whites that they have sold their lands and divided the money. But this only happens when the Indians ask for it. Treaties last forever, as signed, unless the Indians wish to make a change. I understand you all agree to the terms of the Treaty. Am I right? If so, I will have the Treaty drawn up, and to-morrow we will sign it. Speak, all those who do not agree!"

Moostoos: " I agree."

Keenooshayo: " My children, all who agree, stand up!"

The Reverend Father Lacombe then addressed the Indians in substance as follows: He reminded them that he was an old friend, and came amongst them seven years ago, and, being now old, he came again to fulfil another duty, and to assist the Commission to make a treaty. " Knowing you as I do, your manners, your customs and language, I have been officially attached to the Commission as adviser. To-day is a great day for you, a day of long remembrance, and your children hereafter will learn from your lips the events of to-day. I consented to come here because I thought it was a good thing for you to take the Treaty. Were it not in your interest I would not take part in it. I have been long familiar with the Government's methods of making treaties with the Saulteaux of Manitoba, the Crees of Saskatchewan, and the Blackfeet, Bloods and Piegans of the Plains, and advised these tribes to accept the offers of the Government. Therefore, to-day, I urge you to accept the words of the Big Chief who comes here in the name of the Queen. I have known him for many years, and, I can assure you, he is just and sincere in all his statements, besides being vested with authority to deal with you. Your forest and river life will not be changed by the Treaty, and you will have your annuities, as well, year by year, as long as the sun shines and the earth remains. Therefore I finish my speaking by saying, Accept!"

The chiefs and counsellors stood up, and requested all the Indians to do so also as a mark of acceptance of the Government's conditions. Father Lacombe was thanked by

several for having come so far, though so very old, to visit
them and speak to them, after which the meeting adjourned
until the following day.

At three p.m. on Wednesday, the 21st, the discussion was
resumed by Mr. Laird, who, after a few preliminary
remarks, read the Treaty, which had been drafted by the
Commissioners the previous evening. Chief Keenooshayo
arose and made a speech, followed by Moostoos, both assent-
ing to the terms, when suddenly, and to the surprise of all,
the chief, who had again begun to address the Indians, per-
ceiving gestures of dissent from his people, suddenly stopped
and sat down. This looked critical; but, after a somewhat
lengthy discussion, everything was smoothed over, and the
chief and head men entered the tent and signed the Treaty
after the Commissioners, thus confirming, for this portion
of the country, the great Treaty which is intended to cover
the whole northern region up to the sixtieth parallel of north
latitude. The satisfactory turn of the Lesser Slave Lake
Treaty, it was felt, would have a good effect elsewhere, and
that, upon hearing of it at the various treaty points to the
west and north, the Indians would be more inclined to
expedite matters, and to close with the Commissioner's
proposals.*

The text of the Treaty itself, which may be of interest to
the reader, will be found in full in the Appendix, page 471.

The first and most important step having been taken, the
other essential adhesions had now to be effected. To save
time and wintering in the country, the Treaty Commission
separated, Messrs. Ross and McKenna leaving on the 22nd

---

*The foregoing report of the Treaty discussions is necessarily
much abridged, being simply a transcript of brief notes taken at the
time. The utterances particularly of Keenooshayo, but also of his
brother, were not mere harangues addressed to the "groundlings,"
but were grave statements marked by self-restraint, good sense and
courtesy, such as would have done no discredit to a well-bred
white man. They furthered affairs greatly, and in two days the
Treaty was discussed and signed, in singular contrast with treaty-
making on the plains in former years.

Mr. Laird addressing the Beavers and Crees at Fort Vermilion

for Fort Dunvegan and St. John, whilst Mr. Laird set out
shortly afterwards for Vermilion and Fond du Lac, on Lake
Athabasca.   He reached Peace River Crossing on the 30th,
and met there, next day, a few Beaver Indians and the Crees
of the region.   The Beaver chief, who was present, did not
adhere, saying that his band was at Fort Dunvegan, and
that he could not get there in time.   The date of the St. John
Treaty had been fixed for the 21st of June, but, owing to
the detentions described, the appointment could not be kept,
and word was therefore sent to the Indians to stay where
they were until they could be met.   But when the Commissioners were within twenty-five miles of the Fort they got
a letter from the Hudson's Bay Company's agent telling
them that the Indians had eaten up all the provisions there,
and had left for their hunting-grounds, with no hope of their
coming together again that season.   They therefore returned
to Fort Dunvegan, and took the adhesion of some Beaver
Indians, and then left for Lower Peace River.   On the 8th
July, Mr. Laird secured the adhesion of the Crees and
Beavers at Fort Vermilion, and Messrs. Ross and McKenna
of those at Little Red River, the headman there refusing to
sign at first because, he said, " he had a divine inspiration
to the contrary "!   This was followed by adhesions taken by
the latter Commissioners, on the 13th, from the Crees and
Chipewyans at Fort Chipewyan.

   " Here it was," Mr. McKenna writes me, " that the chief
asked for a railway—the first time in the history of Canada
that the red man demanded as a condition of cession that
steel should be laid into his country.   He evidently understood the transportation question, for a railway, he said, by
bringing them into closer connection with the market, would
enhance the value of what they had to sell, and decrease the
cost of what they had to buy.   He had a striking object-
lesson in the fact that flour was $12 a sack at the Fort.
These Chipewyans lost no time in flowery oratory, but came
at once to business, and kept us, myself in particular, on

5

tenterhooks for two hours. I never felt so relieved as when the rain of questions ended, and, satisfied by our answers, they acquiesced in the cession."

Next morning these Commissioners left for Smith's Landing, and, on the 17th, made treaty with the Indians of Great Slave Lake. Meanwhile Mr. Laird had proceeded to Fond du Lac, at the eastern end of Lake Athabasca, and there, on the 27th, the Chipewyans adhered, whilst Messrs. Ross and McKenna, in order to treat with the Indians at Fort McMurray and Wahpooskow, separated. The latter secured the Chipewyans and Crees at the former post, and Mr. Ross the Crees at Wahpooskow, both adjustments, by a coincidence, being made on the same day.

This completed the Treaty of 1889, known as No. 8, the most important of all since the Great Treaty of 1876.

The work of the Commission being now over, its members prepared to leave the country. Messrs. Ross and McKenna set out for Athabasca Landing, whilst Mr. Laird accompanied us to Pelican Rapids, but left us there and pushed on, like the others, for home.

There were, of course, many Indians who did not or could not turn up at the various treaty points that year, viz., the Beavers of St. John, the Crees of Sturgeon Lake, the Slaves of Hay River, who should have come to Vermilion, and the Dog-Ribs, Yellow-Knives, Slaves, and Chipewyans, who should have been treated with at Fort Resolution, on Great Slave Lake.

Accordingly, a special commission was issued to Mr. J. A. Macrae, of the Indian Office in Ottawa, who met the Indians the following year at the points named, and in May, June, and July, secured the adhesion of over 1,200 souls, making, with subsequent adhesions, a total of 3,568 souls to the 30th June, 1906.

The largest numbers were at Forts Resolution, Vermilion, Fond du Lac, and Lesser Slave Lake, the latter ranking fourth in the list. Of course, there are still to be treated with the Indians of the Mackenzie River and the Esquimaux of the Arctic coast. But Treaty Eight covers the most valuable portions of the Northern Anticlinal, though this is a conjecture, as the resources of the lower Mackenzie Basin, and even of the Barren Lands, are only now becoming known, and may yet prove to be of great value. Bishop Grouard told me that at their Mission at Fort Providence, potatoes, turnips and barley ripened, and also wheat when tried, though this, he thought, was uncertain. I have also heard Chief-factor Camsell speak quite boastfully of his tomatoes at Fort Simpson. As a matter of fact, little is known practically as to the bearing of the climate and long summer sunshine on agriculture in the Mackenzie District. But be that region what it may, there has been already ceded an empire in itself, extending, roughly speaking, from the 54th to the 60th parallel of north latitude, and from the 106th to the 130th degree of west longitude. In this domain there is ample room for millions of people; and, as I must now return to the Half-breed Commission on Lesser Slave Lake, I shall give, as we go, as fair a picture as I can of its superficial features and the inducements it offers to the immigrant.

CHAPTER IV.

THE HALF-BREED SCRIP COMMISSION.

The adjustment with the half-breeds depended, of course, upon a successful treaty with the Indians, and, this having been concluded, the latter at once, upon receipt of their payments, left for their forests and fisheries, leaving the half-breeds in full possession of the field.

It was estimated that over a hundred families were encamped around us, some in tepees, some in tents, and some in the open air, the willow copses to the north affording shelter, as well, to a few doubtful members of Slave Lake society, and to at least a thousand dogs. The "scrip tent," as it was called, a large marquee fitted up as an office, had been pitched with the other tents when the camp was made, and in this the half-breeds held a crowded meeting to talk over the terms, and to collate their own opinions as to the form of scrip issue they most desired. In this they were singularly unanimous, and, in spite of advice to the contrary urged upon them in the strongest maner by Father Lacombe, they agreed upon "the bird in the hand"—viz., upon cash scrip or nothing. This could be readily turned into money, for in the train of traders, etc., who followed up the treaty payments, there were also buyers from Winnipeg and Edmonton, well supplied with cash, to purchase all the scrip that offered, at a great reduction, of course, from face value. Whether the half-breeds were wise or foolish it is needless to say. One thing was plain, they had made up their minds. Under the circumstances it was impossible to gainsay their assertion that they were the best judges of their own needs.

Half-breed Commission tent at Lesser Slave Lake

The Commission at work

Scene in the Scrip marquee at Lesser Slave Lake. Note the smart Half-breed
girls to the left and the old-fashioned mother near them

All preliminaries having at last been settled, the taking of declarations and evidence began on the 23rd of June, and, shortly afterwards, the issue of convertible scrip certificates, or scrip certificates for land as required, took place to the parties who had proved their title.

This was a slow process, involving in every case a careful search of the five elephant folios containing the records of the bygone issues of scrip in Manitoba and the organized Territories.

It was necessary in order to prevent the issue of scrip to parties who had already received it elsewhere. But to the credit of the Lesser Slave Lake community, few efforts were made to " come in " again, not one in fact which was a clear attempt at fraud, or which could not be accounted for by false agency. Indeed, a high tribute might well be paid here to the honesty, not only of this but of all the communities, both Indian and half-breed, throughout these remote territories. We found valuable property exposed everywhere, evidently without fear of theft. There was a looser feeling regarding debts to traders, which we were told were sometimes ignored, partly, perhaps, owing to the traders' heavy profits, but mainly through failure in the hunt and a lack of means. But theft such as white men practice was a puzzle to these people, amongst whom it was unknown.

The most noticeable feature of the scrip issue was the never-ending stream of applicants, a surprising evidence of the growth of population in this remote wilderness. Its most interesting feature lay in the peculiarities and manners of the people themselves. They were unquestionably half-breeds, and had received Christian names, and most of them had houses of their own, and, though hunters, fishermen and trippers, their families lived comparatively settled lives. Yet the glorious instinct of the Indian haunted them. As a rule they had been born on the " pitching-track," in the forest, or on the prairies—in all sorts of places, they could

not say exactly where—and when they were born was often
a matter of doubt as well.* It was not in February, but in
Meeksuo pésim, " The month when the eagles return "; not in
August, but in Oghpáho pésim, " The month when birds begin
to fly." When called upon they could give their Christian
names and answer to William or Magloire, to Mary or Mada-
line, but, in spite of priest or parson, their home name was
a Cree one. In many cases the white forefather's name had
been dropped or forgotten, and a Cree surname had taken
its place, as, for example, in the name Louis Maskegósis, or
Madeline Nooškeyah. Some of the Cree names were in their
meaning simply grotesque. Mishoóstiquan meant " The
man who stands with the red hair "; Waupunékapow, " He

*With reference to these nondescript birthplaces, the wonderful
ease of parturition among Indian women may be referred to here.
This is common, probably, to all primitive races, but is perhaps
more marked amongst Indian mothers than any other. The event
may happen in a canoe, on the trail, at any place, or at any moment,
without hindering the ordinary progress of a travelling party, which
is generally overtaken by the mother in a few hours. But nothing
I heard here equalled in grotesque circumstances occurrences, whose
truth I can vouch for, many years ago on the Saskatchewan River.
In 1874, if I remember aright, a great spring freshet in the North
Branch was accompanied by a tremendous ice-jam, which backed
the water up, and flooded the river bank so suddenly that many
Indians were drowned. On an island below Prince Albert, a woman,
to save her life, had to climb a neighbouring tree, and gave birth to
a child amongst the branches. The jam broke, and, wonderful to
say, both mother and child got down to firm ground alive. Another
case, even more gruesome, happened on the Lower Saskatchewan
not so many years ago. A woman and her husband were hastening
on snowshoes from their winter camp to the river, in order to share
in the usual Christmas bounty and festivities at the Hudson's Bay
Company's post. The woman was seized with incipient labour, and,
darting from her husband, with whom she had been quarrelling on
the way, pushed on, and, in a frozen marsh, amongst bulrushes, on
a bitterly cold night, was delivered of a child. Grumous as she was,
she picked herself up, and, with incredible nerve, walked ten miles
to the Pas, carrying her live infant with her, wrapped in a rabbit-
skin robe.

who stands till morning." One of the applicants was Kanawatchaguáyo, or "The ghost-keeper."*

But others were strikingly poetical, particularly the female
names. Payúcko geesigo, "One in the Skies"; Pesawakoona
kapesisk, "The silent snow in falling forming signs or
symbols"; Matyatse wunoguayo, or rather, for this is a
doubtful name, Powástia ka nunaghquánetungh, "Listener to
the unseen rapids"; Kese koo ápeoo, "She sits in Heaven,"
were all the names of applicants for scrips, and many others
could be added of like tenor. In a word, the Christian or
baptismal names have not displaced the native ones, as
they did in Wales and elsewhere, and amongst some of
our far Eastern Indians. But there were terrifying and
repulsive names as well, such as Sese kenápik kaow
apeoo, "She sits like a rattle-snake"; and one individual rejoiced in the appalling surname of "Grand
Bastard." These instances serve to illustrate the tendency of half-breed nomenclature at the lake towards the
mother's side. Here, too, there was no reserve in giving the
family name; it was given at once when asked for, and there
was no shyness otherwise in demeanour. There was a readiness, for example, to be photographed which was quite distinctive. In this connection it may interest the reader to
recall some of the names of girls given by the same race
thousands of miles away in the East. Take those recorded
by Mrs. Jameson† during her visit to Mrs. McMurray and
the Schoolcrafts, on the Island of Mackinac, over seventy

---

*It may be mentioned here that this half-breed's "inner" name,
so to speak, meant "The Ghost-Keeper," for the name he gave,
following an Indian usage, was not the real one. Kanawatchaguáyo
was the one given by the interpreter, but accompanied by the·trans-
lation of the inner name, to wit, "The Ghost-Keeper." This curious
custom is more fully referred to in a forthcoming work on Indian
folk-lore, traditions, legends, usages, methods and manner of life,
etc., by Mrs. F. H. Paget, of Ottawa. This lady is an expert Cree
scholar, and her work, which I have had the pleasure of hearing
her read, is the result of diligent research and of ample knowledge
of Indian life and character.

† "Winter Studies and Summer Rambles," 1835.

years ago: Oba baumwawa geezegoquay, "The Sounds which the stars make rushing through the skies"; Zaga see goquay, "Sunbeams breaking through a cloud"; Waḣsagewanoquay, "Woman of the bright foam." The people so far apart, yet their home names so similarly figurative! The education of the Red Indian lies in his intimate contact with nature in all her phases—a good education truly, which serves him well. But, awe-struck always by the mysterious beauty of the world around him, his mind reflects it instinctively in his Nature-worship and his system of names.

In speaking of the "Lakers" I refer, of course, to the primitive people of the region, and not to half-breed incomers from Manitoba or elsewhere. There were a few patriarchal families into which all the others seemed to dovetail in some shape or form. The Noóskeyah family was one of these, also the Gladu, the Cowitoreille,* and the Calahaisen. The collateral branches of these families constituted the main portion of the native population, and yet inbreeding did not seem to have deteriorated the stock, for a healthier-looking lot of young men, women and children it would be hard to find, or one more free from scrofula. There were instances, too, among these people, of extreme old age; one in particular which from confirmatory evidence, particularly the declarations of descendants, seemed quite authentic. This was a woman called Catherine Bisson—the daughter of Baptiste Bisson and an Indian woman called Iskwao—who was born on New Year's Day, 1793, at Lesser Slave Lake, and had spent all her life there since. She had a numerous progeny which she bore to Kisiśkakápo, "The man who stands still." She was now blind, and was partly led, partly carried into our tent—a small, thin, wizened woman, with keen features and a tongue as keen, which cackled and joked at a great rate with the crowd around her. It was almost awesome to look at this weird piece of antiquity, who was born in the Reign of Terror, and was a young woman before

---

* A corruption, no doubt, of "Courtoreille."

the war of 1812. She was quite lively yet, so far as her wits went, and seemed likely to go on living.*

There were many good points in the disposition of the "Lakers" generally, both young and old. Their kindness and courtesy to strangers and to each other was marked, and profanity was unknown. Indeed, if one heard bad language at all it was from the lips of some Yankee or Canadian teamster, airing his superior knowledge of the world amongst the natives.

The place, in fact, surprised one—no end of buggies, buckboards and saddles, and brightly dressed women, after a not altogether antique fashion; the men, too, orderly, civil, and obliging. Infants were generally tucked into the comfortable moss-bag, but boys three or four years old were seen tugging at their mothers' breasts, and all fat and generally good-looking. The whole community seemed well fed, and were certainly well clad—some girls extravagantly so, the love of finery being the ruling trait here as elsewhere. One lost, indeed, all sense of remoteness, there was such a well-to-do, familiar air about the scene, and such a bustle of clean-looking people. How all this could be supported by fur it was difficult to see, but it must have been so, for there was, as yet, little or no farming amongst the old "Lakers." It was, of course, a great fur country, and though the fur-bearing animals were sensibly diminishing, yet the prices of peltries had risen by competition, whilst supplies had been correspondingly cheapened. It was a good marten country, and, as this fur was the fad of fashion, and brought an extravagant price, the animal, like the beaver, was threatened with extinction, the more so as the rabbits were then in their period of scarcity.

There were other aspects of Lake life which there is neither space nor inclination to describe. If some features

---

*This very old woman died, I believe, at Lesser Slave Lake only last spring (1908). If the date of her birth was correct, and we had good reason to believe it, she must have been far over 100 years old when she died.

of " advanced civilization " had been anticipated there, it was simply another proof that extremes meet.

Whatever else was hidden, however, there was one thing omnipresent, namely, the mongrel dog. It was hopeless to explore the origin of an animal which seemed to draw from all sources, including the wolf and fox, and whose appetite stopped at nothing, but attacked old shirts, trousers, dunnage-bags, fry-pans, and even the outfit of a geologist, to appease the sacred rage of hunger.

It was believed that over a thousand of these dogs, mainly used in winter to haul fish, surrounded our tent, and when it is said that an ordinary half-breed family harboured from fifteen to twenty of the tribe, there is no exaggeration in the estimate. They were of all shapes, sizes and colours, and, though very civil to man, from whom they got nothing but kicks and stones, they kept up a constant row amongst themselves.

To see a scrimmage of fifty or sixty of them on land or in the water, where they went daily to fish, was a scene to be remembered. They did not bark, but loped through the woods, which were the camp's latrines, as scavengers by day, and howled in unison at regular intervals by night; for there was a sort of horrible harmony in the performance, and when the tom-toms of the gamblers accompanied it on all sides, and the pounding of dancers' feet—for in this enchanted land nobody ever seemed to go to bed—the saturnalia was complete.

It was indeed a gala time for the happy-go-lucky Lakers, and the effects of the issue and sale of scrip certificates were soon manifest in our neighbourhood. The traders' booths were thronged with purchasers, also the refreshment tents where cigars and ginger ale were sold; and, in tepees improvised from aspen saplings, the sporting element passed the night at some interesting but easy way of losing money, illuminating their game with guttering candles, minus candlesticks, and presenting a picture worthy of an impressionist's pencil.

But the two dancing floors were the chief attraction. These also had been walled and roofed with leafy saplings, their fronts open to the air, and, thronged as they generally were, well repaid a visit. Here the comely brunettes, in moccasins or slippers, their luxuriant hair falling in a braided queue behind their backs, served not only as tireless partners, but as foils to the young men, who were one and all consummate masters of step-dancing, an art which, I am glad to say, was still in vogue in these remote parts. "French-fours" and the immortal "Red River Jig" were repeated again and again, and, though a tall and handsome young half-breed, who had learned in Edmonton, probably, the airs and graces of the polite world, introduced cotillons and gave "the calls" with vigorous precision, yet his efforts were not thoroughly successful. Snarls arose, and knots and confusion, which he did his best to undo. But it was evident that the hearts of the dancers were not in it. No sooner was the fiddler heard lowering his strings for the time-honoured "Jig" than eyes brightened, and feet began to beat the floor, including, of course, those of the fiddler himself, who put his whole soul into that weird and wonderful melody, whose fantastic glee is so strangly blended with an indescribable master-note of sadness. The dance itself is nothing; it might as well be called a Rigadoon or a Sailor's Hornpipe, so far as the steps go. The tune is everything; it is amongst the immortals. Who composed it? Did it come from Normandy, the ancestral home of so many French Canadians and of French Canadian song? Or did some lonely but inspired voyageur, on the banks of Red River, sighing for Detroit or Trois Rivières—for the joys and sorrows of home—give birth to its mingled chords in the far, wild past?

As I looked on, many memories recurred to me of scenes like this in which I had myself taken part in bygone days— *Eheu! fugaces*—in old Red River and the Saskatchewan; and, with these in my heart, I retired to my tent, and gradually fell asleep to the monotonous sound of the familiar yet inexplicable air.

CHAPTER V.

RESOURCES OF LESSER SLAVE LAKE REGION.

I⊤ was expected that the sergeant of the Mounted Police stationed at the Lake would have set out by boat on the 3rd for Athabasca Landing, taking with him the witnesses in the Weeghteko case—a case not common amongst the Lesser Slave Lake Indians, but which was said to be on the increase. One Pahayo—" The Pheasant "—had gone mad and threatened to kill and eat people. Of course, this was attributed by his tribe to the Weeghteko, by which he was believed to be possessed, a cannibal spirit who inhabits the human heart in the form of a lump of ice, which must be got rid of by immersion of the victim in boiling water, or by pouring boiling fat down his throat. This failing, they destroy the man-eater, rip him up to let out the evil spirit, cut off his head, and then pin his four quarters to the ground, all of which was done by his tribe in the case of Pahayo. Napesósus —" The Little Man "—struck the first blow, Moostoos followed, and the poor lunatic was soon dispatched. Arrests were ultimately made, and a boatload of witnesses was about to leave for Athabasca Landing, *en route* to attend the trial at Edmonton, the first of its kind, I think, on record.

There can be no doubt that such slayings are effected to safeguard the tribe. Indians have no asylums, and, in order to get a dangerous lunatic out of the way, can only kill him. There would therefore be no hangings. But, now that the Indians and ourselves were coming under treaty obligations, it was necessary that an end should be put to such proceedings.

76

Yet the reader must not be too severe upon the Indian for his treatment of the Weeghteko. He attributes the disease to the evil spirit, acts accordingly, and slays the victim. But an old author, Mrs. Jameson, tells us that in her day in Upper Canada lunatics were allowed to stray into the forest to roam uncared for, and perish there, or were thrust into common jails. One at Niagara, she says, was chained up for four years.

Aside from such cases of madness, which have often resulted in the killing and eating of children, etc., and which arouse the most superstitious horror in the minds of all Indians, the " savages " of this region are the most inoffensive imaginable. They have always made a good living by hunting and trapping and fishing, and I believe when the time comes they will adapt themselves much more readily and intelligently to farming and stock-raising than did the Indians to the south. The region is well suited to both industries, and will undoubtedly attract white settlers in due time.

The fisheries in Lesser Slave Lake have always been counted the best in all Athabasca. The whitefish, to be sure, are diminishing towards the head of the lake, but it is possible that this is owing to some deficiency in their usual supply of food in that quarter. Just as birds and wild-fowl return, if not disturbed, to their accustomed breeding-places, so, it is said, the fishes, year by year, drop and impregnate their spawn upon the same gravelly shallows. The food of the whitefish in the lake is partly the worms bred from the eggs of a large fly resembling the May-fly of the East. This worm has probably decreased in the upper part of the lake, and therefore the fish go farther down for food. There they are exceedingly numerous, an evidence of which is the fact that the Roman Catholic Mission alone secured 17,000 fine whitefish the previous fall. Properly protected this lake will be a permanent source of supply to natives and incomers for many years to come.

Stock-raising was already becoming a feature of the region. Some three miles above the Heart River is Buffalo Lake, an enlargement of that stream, and around and above this, as also along the Wyaweekamon, or " Passage between the Lakes," are immense hay meadows, capable of winter feeding thousands of cattle.   The view of these vast meadows from the Hudson's Bay post, or from the Roman Catholic Mission close by, is magnificent.

These buildings are situated above Buffalo Lake, upon a lofty bank, with the Heart River in the foreground; and the great meadows, threaded by creeks and inlets, stretching for miles to the south of them, are one of the finest sights of the kind in the country.

In the far south was the line of forest, and to the eastward a flat-topped mountain, called by the Crees Waskahékum Kahassástakee—" The House Butte."   Near this mountain is the Swan River, which joins the Lesser Slave Lake below the Narrows, and upon which, we were told, were rich and extensive prairies, and abundance of coal of a good quality. To the west were the prairies of the Salt River, well watered by creeks, with a large extent of good land now being settled on, and where wheat ripens perfectly.

There are other available areas of open country on Prairie River, which enters Buffalo Lake at its south-western end, and on which also there is coal, so that prairie land is not entirely lacking.

Though emphatically *now* a region of forest, there is reason to believe that vast areas at present under timber were once prairies, fed over by innumerable herds of buffalo, whose paths and wallows can still be traced in the woods.   Indeed, very large trees are found growing right across those paths, and this fact, not to speak of the recollections, or traditions, of very old people, points to extensive prairies at one time rather than to an entirely wooded country.

Much of the forest soil is excellent, and the land has only to be cleared to furnish good farms.   Indeed, it needs no

stretch of imagination to foresee in future years a continuous
line of them from Edmonton to the lake, along the three
hundred miles of country intersected by the trail laid out
by the Territorial Government.

As for the wheat problem, it is not at all likely that the
Roman Catholic Mission would put up a flour mill, as they
were then doing, if it was not a wheat country. Bishop Clût
assured me that potatoes in their garden reached three and a
half pounds' weight in some instances, and turnips twenty-
five pounds.

The kind people of both this and the Church of England
Mission generously supplied our table with vegetables and
salads, and we craved no better. Chives, lettuce, radishes,
cress and onions were full flavoured, fresh and delicious, and
quite as early as in Manitoba. Being a timber country, lumber was, of course, plentiful, there being two sawmills at
work cutting lumber, which sold, undressed, at $25 to $30 a
thousand.

The whole country has a fresh and attractive look, and one
could not desire a finer location than can be had almost anywhere along its streams and within its delightful and healthy
borders. And yet this region is but a portal to the vaster
one beyond, to the Unjigah, the mighty Peace River, to be
described hereafter.

The make-weight against settlement may be almost summed
up in the words transport and markets. The country is
there, and far beyond it, too; but so long as there is abundance of prairie land to the south, and no railway facilities,
it would be unwise for any large body of settlers, especially
with limited means, to venture so far. The small local
demand for beef and grain might soon be overtaken, and
though stock can be driven, yet three hundred miles of forest
trail is a long way to drive. Still, pioneers take little thought
of such conditions, and already they were dropping in in
twos and threes as they used to do in the old days in Red
River Settlement, lured by the wilderness perhaps to priva-

tion, but entering a country much of which is suited by nature for the support of man.

The best reflection is that there is a really good country to fall back upon when the prairies to the south are taken up. Swamps and muskegs abound, but good land also abounds, and the time will come when the ring of the Canadian axe will be heard throughout these forests, and when multitudes of comfortable homes will be hewn out of what are the almost inaccessible wildernesses of to-day.

By the end of the first week in July the issue of scrip certificates began to fall off, though the declarations were still numerous. But land was in sight; that is to say, our release and departure for Peace River, which we were all very anxious, in fact burning, to see.

By this time there was, of course, much money afloat amongst the people, which was rapidly finding its way into the traders' pockets. There was a " blind pig," too, doing business in the locality, though we could not discover where, as everybody professed entire ignorance of anything of the kind. The fragrant breath and hilarity of so many, however, betrayed its existence, and, as a crowning evidence, before sunrise on the 6th, we were all awakened by an uproarious row amongst a tipsy crowd on the common.

The disturbance, of course, awakened the dogs, if, indeed, those wonderful creatures ever slept, and soon a prolonged howl, issuing from a thousand throats, made the racket complete. It seemed to our listening ears, for we stuck to our beds, to be a promiscuous fight, larded with imprecations in broken English, the phrase " goddam " being repeated in the most comical way. We expected to see a lot of badly bruised men in the morning, but nothing of the kind! Nobody was hurt. It proved to be a very bloodless affair, like the scrimmages of the dogs themselves, full of sound and fury signifying nothing.

CHAPTER VI.

ON THE TRAIL TO PEACE RIVER.

By the afternoon of the 12th we had finished our work at
the lake, and in the evening left the scene of so much amuse-
ment, and its lively and intelligent people, not without regret.
Having said good-bye to Bishop Clût and his clergy, and to
the Hudson's Bay Company's people, and others, we passed
on to Salt Creek, which we crossed at dusk, and then to the
South Heart River—Otaye Sepe—where we camped for the
night. This affluent of the lake has a broad but sluggish
current, its grassy banks sloping gently to the water's edge,
like some Ontario river—the beau ideal of a pike stream.
The Church of England Mission was established here in
charge of the Reverend Mr. Holmes, who had shown us every
kindness during our long stay. As boats can ascend in high
water to this point, the Hudson's Bay Company had a couple
of large warehouses close by, standing alone, and filled with
all kinds of goods. The trail led for many miles up a long,
easy ascent, through a timber country, to an upper plateau,
with, after passing the Heart River, occasional small patches
of prairie on the wayside. The plateau itself is the anticlinal
down which the North Heart flows to Peace River, which it
joins at the crossing.

The trail so far had been good, but after crossing Slippery
Creek it proved to be almost a continuous mud-hole, due to
its extreme narrowness and the wet weather, closely bordered, as much of it was, by dense forests. It revealed a
good farming country, however, free from stones, and the
soil a rich, loamy clay throughout. It was well timbered, in
some places, with the finest white poplar I had yet seen.

The grass was luxuriant, and the region teemed with tiger-lilies, yarrow, and the wild rose.

The Little Prairie, as it is called, is really a lovely region, in appearance resembling the Saskatchewan country. There was an old Hudson's Bay cattle station here, at that time deserted, and here, too, we were charmed with a mirage of indescribable beauty, an enchanting portal to the mighty Peace, which we reached about mid-day on the 15th of July.

The view up the Peace River from the high prairie level is singularly beautiful, the river disclosing a series of reaches, like inland lakes, far to the west, whilst from the south comes the immense valley of the Heart, and, farther up, the Smoky River, a great tributary which drains a large extent of prairie country mixed with timber.

To the north spreads upward, and backward to its summit, the vast bank of the river, varied as to surface by rounded bare hills and valleys and flats sprinkled with aspens, cherries, and saskatoons, the latter loaded with ripe fruit.

The banks of the Peace River are a country in themselves, in which, particularly on the north side, numerous home-steads might be, and indeed have been, carved out. Descending to the river, we found a Hudson's Bay Company and Police post. The river here is about a third of a mile wide, and was in freshet, with a current, we thought, of about six miles an hour.

At Smoky River we met a couple of prospectors, Mr. Tryon, a nephew of the ill-fated Admiral, and Mr. Cooper Blachford, down from the Poker Flat mining-camp, this side the Finlay Rapids, in the Selwyn Mountains. They reached that camp by way of Ashcroft, B.C., in twenty-two days, the Peace River route being very much longer and more difficult. They described the camp there as a promising one, with much gold-bearing quartz in sight, but the cost of provisions and the extreme difficulty of development under the circumstances held it back.

There being but a few half-breeds here, we crossed the

The north bank at Peace River Crossing

Commission and half-breeds at Fort Dunvegan, Upper Peace River

Our camp at Peace River Crossing

river, and decided to go on to Fort Dunvegan, and on our
return complete our scrip issue at the Landing; so, partly on
horseback and partly by waggon, we made our way to our
first camp.   The trail lay along and up and down the
immense bank of the river, debouching at one place at the
site of old Fort McLeod, and passing the fine St. Germain
farm, with as beautiful fields of yellowing wheat as one
would wish to see.

Here we got an abundant supply of vegetables, and in this
ride our first taste of the Peace River mosquito—or, rather,
that animal got its first taste of us.   It is needless to dwell
upon this pest.   Like the fleas in Italy, it has been overdone
in description, and yet beggars it.

All along the trail were old buffalo paths and wallows.
Indeed, we saw them everywhere we went on land, showing
how numerous those animals were in times past.   In 1793
Sir Alexander Mackenzie describes them as grazing in great
numbers along these very banks, the calves frisking about
their dams, and moose and red deer were equally numerous.
In 1828 Sir George Simpson made a canoe journey to the
Coast by way of this river, and they were still very numerous.
The existing tradition is that, some sixty years ago, a winter
occurred of unexampled severity and depth of snow, in
which nearly all the herds perished, and never recovered
their footing on the upper river.   The wood buffalo still
exists on Great Slave River, but, where we were, the only
memorials of the animal were its paths and wallows, and its
bones half-buried in the fertile earth.

On the morning of the 17th we topped the crest of the
bank, and found ourselves at once in a magnificent prairie
country, which swept northward, varied by beautiful belts
of timber, as far as Bear Lake, to which we made a detour,
then westerly to Old Wives Lake—Nootoóquay Sakaigon—
and on to our night camp at Burnt River, twenty-two miles
from Dunvegan.   The great prairie is as flat as a table, and
is the exact counterpart of Portage Plains, in Manitoba, or

a number of them, with the addition of belts and beautiful islands of timber, the soil being a loamy clay, unmistakably fertile. Nothing could excel the beauty of this region, not even the fairest portions of Manitoba or Saskatchewan.

On the 18th we finished our drive over a like beautiful prairie, slightly rolling, dotted with similar clumps of timber like a great park, and carpeted with ripe strawberries and flowers, including the wild mignonette, the lupin, and the phlox.

Descending a very long and crooked ravine, we reached the river flat at last, upon which is situated Fort Dunvegan, called after the stronghold of the McLeods of Skye, but alas! with no McCrimmon to welcome us with his echoing pipes! Chief-factor McDonald, in his scanty journal of Sir George Simpson's canoe voyage in 1828 from Hudson's Bay to the Pacific, does not give the date at which this post was established, but mentions its abandonment in 1823, owing to the murder of a Mr. Hughes and four men at Fort St. John by the Beaver Indians. It had been re-established by Chief-trader Campbell. Simpson, Mr. McDonald, and Mr. McGillivray, who had embarked at Fort Chipewyan, where Sir George himself had served his clerkship, spent a day at Dunvegan in August, resting and getting fresh supplies. The warring traders had united in 1821, and this voyage was undertaken in order to harmonize the Indians, who, from the bay to the coast, particularly across the mountains, had become fierce partisans of one or other of the great companies.

Sir George had his McCrimmon with him in the shape of his piper, Colin Fraser, who played and paraded before the Indians most impressively in full Highland costume. Deer and buffalo were numerous in the region, and, during the day, thirteen sacks of pemmican were made for the party from materials stored at the fort. Simpson was famous in those days for his swift journeys with his celebrated Iroquois canoemen. They were made by *Canot du Maitre,* as it was called, the largest bark canoe made by the Indians, carrying about six tons and a crew of sixteen paddlers, and which ascended as far as Fort William.   Thence further progress was made in the much smaller " North Canoes " to all points west of Lake Superior.   This particular journey of nearly 3,200 miles, made almost entirely by canoe, was completed from York Factory to Fort Langley, near the mouth of Fraser River, in sixty-five days of actual paddling, an average of about fifty miles a day, nearly all up stream.

Only two buildings of the old fort remained at the time of our visit, both in a ruinous condition.   The old fireplaces and the roofs of spruce bark, a covering much used in the country, were still sound, and several cellars indicated where the other buildings had stood.   The later post is about a gun-shot to the east of them, and the whole site had certainly been well chosen, being completely sheltered by the immensely high banks of the great and deep river, whose bends " shoul-dered " and seemed to shut in the place east and west, also by the " Caps," two very high hills forming the bank on each side of the river, so called from their fancied resemblance to a skull-cap.   The river here is over four hundred yards in width, and its banks, from the water's edge to the upper prairie level, are some six hundred feet or more in height; but, as the trail leads, the ascent of the great slope is about a mile in length.

A number of townships had been blocked here, at one time, by Mr. Ogilvie, D.L.S., but not subdivided, Fort Dun-vegan being situated, if I mistake not, in the south-west corner of Township 80, Range 4, west of the Sixth Meridian.

The Roman Catholic Mission east of the fort was found to be beautifully sheltered, and neighboured by fine fields of wheat and a garden full of green peas and new potatoes.   But this was on the flat.   There was no farming whatever on the north side, on the upper and beautiful prairies described.   A Mr. Milton had tried, it was said, about ten miles east of Dunvegan, but did not make a success of it.

Near the fort a raft was moored, on which had descended a party of four Americans. They were from the State of Wyoming, and had made their way the previous summer, by way of St. John and the Pine River, to the Nelson, a tributary of the Liard. They had had poor luck, in fact no luck at all; and this was the story of every returning party we met which had been prospecting on the various tributaries of the Peace and Liard towards the mountains. The cost of supplies, the varying and uncertain yield, but, above all, the brief season in which it is possible to work—barely six weeks —had dissipated by sad experience the bright dreams of wealth which had lured them from comfortable homes. Between seven and eight hundred people had gone up to those regions *via* Edmonton, bound for the Yukon, many of whom, after a tale of suffering which might have filled its boomsters' souls with remorse, had found solitary graves, and the remainder were slowly toiling out of the country, having sunk what means they possessed in the vain pursuit of gold. They brought a rumour with them that some whites who had robbed the Indians on the Upper Liard had been murdered. It was not known what white men had penetrated to that desolate region, and the rumour was discredited; at all events, it was never verified.

The treaty had been effected at Dunvegan, on the 6th, with a few Beaver Indians, who still lingered by their tepees, pitched to the west on the opposite shore. The half-breeds had camped near the fort pending our arrival, and we found them a very intelligent people, indeed, with some interesting relics of the old régime still amongst them. One, in particular, had canoed from Lachine with Simpson sixty years before. He was still lively and active, and a patriarch of the half-breed community. Large families we found to be the rule here, some parents boasting of twelve or thirteen children *under* age. This, and their healthy looks, spoke well for the climate, and their condition otherwise was promising, being comfortably clad, all speaking more or less English or French, whilst many could read and write.

Healthy Half Breeds.

Our work being completed here, we set out for the Crossing by waggon, our route lying over the same majestic prairies, and reached the Landing the second night, passing the Roman Catholic and Church of England Missions on the way. The former Mission is an extensive establishment, with a fine farm and garden. Indeed, with the exception of primitive outlying stations, all the principal Roman Catholic Missions, by their extent and completeness, put our own more meagrely endowed establishments into rather painful contrast.

A great concourse of natives was at the Landing awaiting our arrival. The place was covered with tepees and tents, and no less than four trading marquees had been pitched pending the scrip issue, which it took some time to complete.

Near the Landing were the mill and farm of a namesake of Sir Alexander Mackenzie. His father, indeed, was a cousin of the renowned explorer who gave his name to the great river of the North. This father, under whom, Mr. Mackenzie said, Lord Strathcona had spent his first year as a clerk in the Hudson's Bay Company's service, was drowned, with nine Iroquois, whilst running the Lachine Rapids in a bark canoe. His son came to Peace River in 1863, and his career, as he told it to me, will bear repeating. He was born at Three Rivers, in Lower Canada, in 1843, and was sent to Scotland to be educated, remaining there until he was eighteen years of age. In 1861 he joined the Hudson's Bay Company's service, wintering first at Norway House under Chief-factor William Sinclair, but removed to Peace River, became a chief-trader there in 1872, and, after some years of service, retired, and has lived at the Crossing ever since.

The Landing, he told me, used to be known as " The Forks," it being here that the Smoky River joins the Peace; and here were concentrated, in bygone days, the posts and rivalries of the great fur companies. The remains of the North-West Company's fort are still visible on the north bank, a few miles above the Landing. On the south shore, in the angle of the two rivers, stood the Hudson's Bay Company's fort, whilst the old X. Y. Company's post, at that time the best equipped on the river, stood on the north bank opposite the Smoky.

In a delightful afternoon spent in rambling over this interesting neighbourhood, Mr. Mackenzie made out for me the site of the latter establishment, now in the midst of a dense thicket of nettles, shrubs, and saplings. In this locality the antagonisms of old had full play—not only those of the traders, but of the Indians—and the river exhibited much more life and movement then than at the time of our visit.

In remote days a constant warfare had been kept up by the Crees on the river, who, just as they invaded the Blackfeet on the Saskatchewan, encroached here upon the Beavers—at that time a brave, numerous and warlike tribe, but now decayed almost to extinction, the victims, it is said, of incestuous intercourse. The Beavers had also an enemy in their congeners, the Chipewyans, the three nations seemingly dividing the great river between them. But neither succeeded in giving a permanent name to it. The Uṅjigah, its majestic and proper name, or the Tsa-hoo-dene-desay— " The Beaver Indian River "—or the Amiskoo eëinnu Sepe of the Crees, which has the same meaning, has not taken root in our maps. The traditional peace made between its warring tribes gave it its name, the Riviere la Paix of the French, which we have adopted, and by this name the river will doubtless be known when the Indians, whose home it has been for ages, have disappeared.

On the 24th our work here was completed, and we took to our boats, which were to float us down to Vermilion and Athabasca Lake. During our stay, however, I had noted all the information that could be gained respecting the Upper Peace as an agricultural region, some of which I have already given. The knowledge obtainable about the fertile areas of the hinterlands of a vast unsurveyed country like this, though not very ample, was no doubt trustworthy as far as it went.

Trappers and traders are confined to the water, as a rule, and see little land away from the shores of streams and lakes. The only people who, through their employments, knew the interior well were the Indians and half-breed hunters. It was the statements of these, therefore, and of the few prosperous farmers and stockmen scattered here and there, which afforded us our only reliable knowledge.

The most extensive prairies adjacent to the Upper Peace River are those to the north already described. The nearest on the south side are the prairies of Spirit River, a small stream which divides several townships of first-class black, loamy soil, well wooded in parts, but with considerable prairie. The nearest farmer and rancher to Dunvegan, Mr. C. Brymner, who had lived for ten years on Spirit River, told me that during seven of these, though frost had touched his grain, particularly in June, it had done little serious harm. It was a fine hay country, he said, even the ridge hay being good, and therefore a good region for cattle, he himself having at the time over a hundred head, which fed out late in the fall and very early in the spring, owing to the Chinook winds, which enter the region and temper its climate. Southeast of Fort St. John there is a considerable area known as Pooscapee's Prairie, getting its name from an old Indian chief, and which was well spoken of, but which we did not see.

A much more extensive open country, however, is the Grand Prairie, to the south-west of the Crossing, which connects with the Spirit River country, and is drained by the Smoky River and its branches, and by its tributary, the Wapiti. There is no dispute as to whether this should or should not be called a prairie country. As a matter of fact, it is an extensive district suitable for immediate cultivation, and containing, as well, valuable timber for lumber, fencing and building.

The first inquiry the intending immigrant makes is about frost. At the Dunvegan and St. Augustine Mission farms, on the river bank above the Landing, Father Busson told me that White Russian and Red Fyfe wheat had been raised since 1881, and during all these years it had never been seriously injured, whilst the yield had reached as high as thirty-five bushels to the acre. Seeding began about the middle of April, and harvesting about the middle of August. He was of opinion that along the rim of the upper prairie level wheat would ripen, but farther back he thought it unsafe, and so no doubt it is for the present. Mr. Brick's fine farm, opposite the Six Islands, and other farms also, were a success, but, of course, all these were along the river. With regard to the upper level, I heard opinions adverse to Father Busson's, though, like his, conjectural. The inconsiderable height above the sea (Lefroy, I think, puts the upper level at about 1,600 feet), the prolonged sunlight, the whole night being penetrated with it though the sun has set, together with good methods of farming, will no doubt get rid of frost, which strikes here just as it has in every new settlement in Manitoba, and in fact throughout a great portion of the continent.

There were complaints, however, of a worse enemy than frost, namely, drought, which we were told was a characteristic feature of those magnificent prairies to the north. The wiry grass is very short there, something like the Milk River grass in Southern Alberta, and hay is scarce. This drawback will doubtless be got over hereafter by dry farming, or better still by irrigation, should the lakes to the north prove to be available.

I have pointed out disadvantages which in all likelihood will disappear with time and settlement by good farmers. It is a region, I believe, predestined to agriculture; but, in some localities, the rainfall, as has been said, is rather scant for good husbandry, and, therefore, farming to the north of the river, on the upper level, is not as yet an assured success. To the south better conditions prevail, and thither no doubt the stream of immigration will first trend.

Altogether we estimated the prairie areas of the upper river at about half a million acres, with much country, in addition, which resembles the Dauphin District in Manitoba, covered with willows and the like, which, if they can be pulled out by horse-power, as is done there, will not be very expensive to clear. There is, of course, any quantity of timber for building and fencing, though much has been destroyed by fire, the varieties being those common to the whole country. To the south, in the Yellowhead, and on the Upper Athabasca and its tributaries, there is considerable prairie also, more easily reached than Peace River; but this is apart from my subject. I may say, in conclusion, that the Upper Peace River country is a very fine one, drained by a vast and navigable river, compared with which the Saskatchewan must yield the palm, and, beyond doubt, this will be the first region to attract settlement and railway development.

Aside from settlers and a railway, the chief needs of the country are a good waggon-road to Edmonton and mail facilities, which were almost non-existent when we were there, but which have recently been to some extent supplied. Nearly three months had elapsed since we entered the country, and not a letter or paper had reached us from the outer world at any point. The imports into the country were increasing very fast, and, through competition and fashion, its principal furs were immensely more valuable than in the past.

As for the natives of the region, we found them a very worthy people, whose progress in the forms of civilized life, and to a certain extent in its elegances, was a constant surprise to us. As for the country, it was plain that all we met were making a good living in it, not by fur alone, but by successful farming, and that its settlement was but a question of time.

CHAPTER VII.

DOWN THE PEACE RIVER.

We had now to descend the river, and our first night in the boats was a bad one. A small but exceedingly diligent variety of mosquito attacked us unprepared; but no ordinary net could have kept them out, anyway. It was a case of heroic endurance, for Beelzebub reigned. The immediate bank of the river was now somewhat low in places, and along it ran a continuous wall, or layer, of sandstone of a uniform height. The stream was vast, with many islands in its course, and whole forests of burnt timber were passed before we reached Battle River, 170 miles down, and which, on the 25th, we left behind us towards evening. Next morning we reached Wolverine Point, a dismal hamlet of six or seven cabins, with a graveyard in their midst. The majority of the half-breeds of the locality had collected here, the others being out hunting. This is a good farming country. Eighteen miles north-west of Paddle River there is a prairie, we were told, of rich black soil, twenty-five miles long and from one to five miles wide, and another south-west of Wolverine, about nine miles in diameter and thirty-six in circumference —clean prairie and good soil, and covered with luxuriant grass and pea-vine. The latter, I think, is watered by a stream called " The Keg," or " Keg of Rum." Wolverine is also a region of heavy spruce timber, and fish are abundant in the various streams which join the Peace River, though not in the Peace itself.

We were now approaching Vermilion, the banks of the river constantly decreasing in height as we descended, until they became quite low. Beneath a waning moon in the south, and an exquisite array of gold and scarlet clouds in the east, which dyed the whole river a delicate red, we floated down to the hamlet of Vermilion. The place proved to be a rather extensive settlement, with yellow wheat-fields and much cattle, for it is a fine hay country. The pioneer Canadians at Vermilion were the Lawrence family, which had been settled there for over twenty years. They were originally residents of Shefford County, Eastern Townships, and set out from Montreal for Peace River in April, 1879, making the journey to Vermilion, by way of Fort Carlton, Isle a la Crosse and Fort McMurray, in four months and some ten days. The elder Mr. Lawrence had been engaged under Bishop Bompas to conduct a mission school at Chipewyan, but after a time removed to Vermilion, where he organized another school, which he conducted until 1891. He then resigned, and began farming on his own account, and, by and by, with great pains and expense, brought in a flour mill, whose operation stimulated settlement, and speedily reduced the price of flour from $25 to $8 a sack. Unfortunately, this useful mill was burnt in April preceding our visit. The yield of grain, moreover, most of it wheat, was estimated at 10,000 bushels, and the burning of the mill was therefore not only a great loss to Mr. Lawrence, but a severe blow to the place. The population interested in farming was estimated at about three hundred souls, thus forming the nucleus of a very promising settlement, now, of course, at its wits' end for gristing. Vermilion seemed to be a very favourable supply point in starting other settlements, being in touch by water with Loon River, Hay River, and other points east and north, where there is abundance of excellent land. For the present, and pending railway development, it was plain that the great and pressing requirement of the region was a good waggon-road by way of Wahpooskow to Athabasca Landing, a distance of three hundred miles, thus avoiding the dangerous rapids of the Athabasca, or the long detour by way of Lesser Slave Lake, and making communication easy in winter time.

From Mr. Erastus Lawrence, the head of the family, we got definite information regarding the region and its prospects for agriculture. We spent Sunday at his comfortable home, and examined his farm carefully. In front of the house was a field of wheat, 110 acres in extent, as fine a field as we had ever seen anywhere, and of this they had not had a failure, he said, during all their farming experience, the return never falling below fourteen bushels to the acre, in the worst of years, twenty-five being about the average yield. They sowed late in April, but reaped generally about the 15th of August. They had never, he said, been seriously injured by frost since 1884, and in fact no frost had occurred to injure wheat since 1887. There was abundance of hay, and 10,000 head of stock, he believed, could be raised at that very point. Many hogs were raised, with great profit, bacon and pork being, of course, high-priced. One of the sons, Mr. E. H. Lawrence, said he had raised sixteen pigs, which at eighteen months dressed 370 pounds apiece. At that time there were about 500 head of cattle, 250 horses, and 200 pigs in the settlement.

After service at the Reverend Mr. Scott's neat little church, we returned to Mr. Lawrence's, and enjoyed an excellent dinner, including home-cured ham, fresh eggs, butter and cream. That was a notable Sunday for us in the wilds, and seldom to be repeated.

Strange to say, we found the true locust here, our old Red River pest, which had quartered itself on the settlement more than once. I examined numbers of them, and found the scarlet egg of the ichneumon fly under many of the shards. No one seemed to know exactly how they came, whether in flight or otherwise; but there they were, devouring some barley, but living mainly upon grass, which they seemed to prefer to grain. They had appeared nine years before our coming, and disappeared, and then, three years before, had come again.

We found quarters in a large building at the fort, which was in charge of Mr. Wilson, whose wife was a daughter of

The Lawrence wheatfield at Fort Vermilion

The beldam of a Cree camp

Ladies of Chipewyan

A primitive R. C. Mission in Athabasca

my old friend, Chief-factor Clarke, of Prince Albert, her brother having charge of the trading store. The post is a substantial one, and the store large, well stocked, and evidently the headquarters of an extensive trade. At such posts, which have generally a fringe of settlement, the Company's officers and their families, though, of course, cut off from the outer world, lead, if somewhat monotonous, by no means irksome lives. Books, music, cards and dances serve to while away spare time, and an occasional wedding, lasting, as it generally does, for several days, stirs the little community to its core. But sport, in a region abounding with game of all kinds, is the great time-killer, giving the longed-for excitement, and contributing as well to the daily bill of fare the very choicest of human food. Such a life is indeed to be envied rather than commiserated, and we met with few, if any, who cared to leave it. But such posts are the " plums " of the service, and are few and far between. At many of the solitary outposts life has a very different colour.*

*" At an outpost," says Mr. Bleasdell Cameron, " where a clerk is alone with his Indian servant, the life is wearisome to a degree, and privation not infrequently adds to the hardship of it. Supplies may run short, and in any case he is expected to stock himself with fish, taken in nets from the lake, near which his post is situated, for his table and his dogs, as well as to augment his larder by the expert and diligent use of his gun. Rare instances have occurred where, through accident, supplies had not reached the far-out posts for which they were intended, and the men had literally died of starvation. Out of a York boat's crew, which was taking up the annual supplies for a post far up among the Rocky Mountains, on a branch of the Mackenzie River, two or three men were drowned, and the ice beginning to take, the boat was obliged to put back to the district headquarters. The three men at the outpost were left for some weeks without the supplies, and when, after winter had set in, and it became possible to reach them with dog trains, and provisions were at length sent them, two were found dead in the post, while the third man was living by himself in a small hut some distance from the fort buildings. The explanation he gave was that he had removed to where there was a chance of keeping himself alive by snaring rabbits, which were more plentiful than at the post. But a suggestion of cannibalism surrounded the affair, for only the bones of his companions were found, and they were in the open chimneyplace. Nothing was done, however, and I myself saw the survivor many times in after years."

At dinner Mr. Wilson told us of a very curious circumstance the previous fall, at the Loon River, some eighty miles south of Vermilion—something, indeed, that very much resembled volcanic action. Indians hunting there were surprised by a great shower of ashes all over the country, thick enough to track moose by, whilst others in canoes were bewildered in dense clouds of smoke. Dr. Wade, a traveller who had just come in from Loon River, said he had discovered three orifices, or " wells," as he called them, out of which he thought the ashes might have been ejected. As there were no forest fires to account for the phenomena, they were rather puzzling.

We had begun taking depositions almost as soon as we arrived, and had a very busy time, working late and early in order to get away by the first of August. There were some interesting people here, " Old Lizotte " and his wife in particular. He was another of the " Ancient Mariners " who had left Lachine fifty-five years before with Governor Simpson—a man still of unshaken nerve and muscles as hard as iron. One by one these old voyageurs are passing away, and with them and their immediate successors the tradition perishes.

There was another character on the Vermilion stage, namely, old King Beaulieu. His father was a half-breed who had been brought up amongst the Dog Ribs and Copper Indians, and some eighty years back had served as an interpreter at Fort Chipewyan. It was he who at Fort Wedderburne sketched for Franklin with charcoal on the floor the route to the Coppermine River, the sketch being completed to and along the coast by Black Meat, an old Chipewyan Indian. King Beaulieu himself was Warburton Pike's right-hand man in his trip to the Barren Lands. He had his own story, of course, about the sportsman, which we utterly discredited. He had joined the Indian Treaty here, but repented, almost flinging his payment in our face, and demanding scrip instead. One of his sons asked me if the law against killing buffalo had not come to an end. I said, " No! the law is stricter than ever—very dangerous now to kill buffalo." Asking him what he thought the band numbered, he said, " About six hundred," and added, " What are we poor half-breeds to do if we cannot shoot them ?" Pointing out the abundance of moose in the country, and that if they shot the buffalo they would soon be exterminated, he still grumbled, and repeated, " What are we poor half-breeds to do ?" I have no doubt whatever that they do shoot them, since the band is reported to have diminished to about 250 head. Immediate steps should certainly be taken to punish and prevent poaching, or this band, the only really wild one on the continent, will soon be extinct.

We were now on our boats again, and heading for the Chutes, as they are called, the one obstruction to the navigation of Peace River for over six hundred miles. We debarked at the head of the rapids above the Grand Fall, and walked to their foot along a shelving and slippery portage, skirting the very edge of the torrent. The Crees call this Meátina Powistik—" The Real Rapid "—the cataract farther on being the Nepegabaketik—" Where the Water Falls."

Returning to the " Decharge," I ran the rapids with Cyr and Baptiste in one of the boats, a glorious sensation, reminding one, though shorter, of the Grand Rapids of the Saskatchewan, the waves being great, and the danger spiced by the tremendous vortex ahead. The rapids are about four hundred yards in length, and extend quite across the river, which is here of an immense width. A heavy but brief rainstorm had set in, and it was some time before we could reload and drop down to the head of the " Chaudiere," if I may call it so, for the vortex much resembles the " Big Kettle " at Ottawa. That night we spent in the York boat, its keel on the rocks and painter tied to a tree, and, lulled by the roar of the cataract, slept soundly until morning.

These falls cut somewhat diagonally across the river, the vortex being at the right bank, and close in-shore, concentred

7

by a limestone shelf extending to the bank, flanked on the left, and at an acute angle, by a deeply-indented reef of rock. Looking up the river, the view to the west seems inclosed by a long line of trees, which, in the distance, appear to stand in the water. Thence the vast stream sweeps boldly into the south, and with a rush discharges down the rapids, and straight over the line of precipice, in a vast tumultuous greyish-drab torrent which speedily emerges into comparatively still water below. The rock here is an exceedingly hard, mottled limestone, resembling the stone at St. Andrew's Rapids on Red River. Where exposed it is pitted or bitten into by the endless action of wind and water, and lies in thick layers, forming an irregular dyke all along the shore, over the surface of which passes the portage, some forty yards in length. Though short, it is a nasty one, running along a shelf of rock into which great gaps have been gored by the torrent. Large quantities of driftwood were stuck in the rapids above, and a big pile of it had lodged at the south angle of the cataract, over which our boats had to be drawn, and dropped down, with great care and difficulty. A rounded, tall island lies, or rather stands, below the falls, towards the north shore, whose sheer escarpments and densely wooded top are very curious and striking. Two sister islands and another above the falls, all four being about a mile apart, stand in line with each other, as if they had once formed parts of an ancient marge, and, below the falls, the torrent has wrought out a sort of bay from the rock, the bank, which is high here, giving that night upon its grassy slope, overhung with dense pine woods, a picturesque camp to our boatmen. The vast river, the rapids and the falls form a majestic picture, not only of material grandeur, but of power to be utilized some day in the service of man. Though formidable, they will yet be surmounted by modern locks; and should Smith's Rapids, on the Great Slave River, be overcome by canalling, there would then be developed one of the longest lines of inland navigation on the continent.

Peace River Rapids

Running the first chute on Peace River

Portaging our boats over the Great Chute of Peace River

The Red River, which joins the Peace about twenty-five miles below the Chutes, flows from the south with a course, it was said, of about two hundred miles, and up this beautiful stream there are extensive prairies. The soil is very rich at the confluence, and we noticed that in the garden at the little Hudson's Bay Company's post, where we transacted our business, vegetables and potatoes were further advanced than at Vermilion, and some ears of wheat were almost ripe. From statements made we judged this to be a region well worth special investigation; it was, in fact, one of the most inviting points for settlement we had seen on our journey.

Following down the Peace, some shoaly places were met with in the afternoon, the banks being low, sandy and uniform, with open woods to the south. The current was stately, but so slow that oars had often to be used. A chilly sunset was followed by an exceedingly brilliant display of Northern Lights, called by the Crees Pahkugh ka Neématchik—"The Dance of the Spirits." This generally presages change; but the day was fine, and next morning we passed what are called the Lower Rapids, below which the banks are lined by precipitous walls of limestone, the river narrowing to less than half of its previous width.

Landing at Peace Point, the traditional scene of the peace between the Beavers and the Chipewyans, or between the Beavers and the Crees, as Mackenzie says, or all three, we found it to be a wide and beautiful table-like prairie, begirt with aspens, on which we flushed a pack of prairie chickens. Below it, and looking upward beyond an island, a line of timber, fringed along the water's edge with willows, sweeps across the view, met half-way by a wall of Devonian rock, whose alternate glitter and shade, in the strong sunshine streaming from the east, seemed almost spectral.

The heavily timbered island added to the effect, and, with a patch of limestone on its cheek, formed a strikingly beautiful foreground.

The only exciting incident of the day was the vigorous

chase, by some of the party, of an old pair of moulting gray geese with their young, all, of course, unable to fly. It was pitiful to watch the clever and fearless actions of the old birds as decoys, falling victims, at last, to parental love. Indeed, they were not worth eating, and to kill them was a sin. But when were there ever scruples over food on Peace River, that theatre of mighty feats of gormandism?

I have already hinted at those masterpieces of voracity for which the region is renowned; yet the undoubted facts related around our camp-fires, and otherwise, a few of which follow, almost beggar belief. Mr. Young, of our party, an old Hudson's Bay officer, knew of sixteen trackers who, in a few days, consumed eight bears, two moose, two bags of pemmican, two sacks of flour, and three sacks of potatoes. Bishop Grouard vouched for four men eating a reindeer at a sitting. Our friend, Mr. d'Eschambault, once gave Oskin-néqu—" The Young Man "—six pounds of pemmican, who ate it all at a meal, washing it down with a gallon of tea, and then complained that he had not had enough. Sir George Simpson states that at Athabasca Lake, in 1820, he was one of a party of twelve who ate twenty-two geese and three ducks at a single meal. But, as he says, they had been three whole days without food. The Saskatchewan folk, however, known of old as the Gens de Blaireaux—" The People of the Badger Holes "—were not behind their congeners. That man of weight and might, our old friend, Chief-factor Belanger—drowned, alas, many years ago with young Simpson at Sea Falls—once served out to thirteen men a sack of pemmican weighing ninety pounds. It was enough for three days; but, there and then, they sat down and consumed it all at a single meal, not, it must be added, without some subsequent and just pangs of indigestion. Mr. B. having occasion to pass the place of eating, and finding the sack of pemmican, as he supposed, in his path, gave it à kick; but, to his amazement, it bounded aloft several yards, and then lit. It was empty! When it is remembered that, in the old buffalo days, the daily

ration per head at the Company's prairie posts was eight
pounds of fresh meat, which was all eaten, its equivalent
being two pounds of pemmican, the enormity of this Gargan-
tuan feast may be imagined. But we ourselves were not bad
hands at the trencher. In fact, we were always hungry. So
I do not reproduce the foregoing facts as a reproach, but
rather as a meagre tribute to the prowess of the great of
old—the men of unbounded stomach!

On the afternoon of the 4th we rounded Point Providence,
the soil exposures sandy, the timber dense but slender, and
early next morning reached the Quatre Fourches, which was
at that time flowing into Lake Athabasca. It is simply a
waterway of some thirty miles in length, which connects
Peace River with the lake, and resembles, in size and colour,
Red River in Manitoba. It is one of " the rivers that turn "
—so called from their reversing their current at different
stages of water. A small stream of this kind connects the
South Saskatchewan with the Qu'Appelle, and another, a
navigable river, the Lower Saskatchewan with Cumberland
Lake. The Quatre Fourches is thus both an inlet and an outlet, but not of the lake in a right sense. The real outlet is
the Rocher River, which joins the Peace River at the inter-
section of latitude 59 with the 111.30th degree of longitude,
beyond which the united streams are called the Great Slave
River.

The Quatre Fourches—" The Four Forks "—gets its name
from the junction of a channel which connects a small lake
called the Mamawee with the south-west angle of Lake Athabasca, Fort Chipewyan being situated on an opposite shore
upon an arm of the lake, here about six miles wide. The
stream is sluggish, and is thickly wooded to the water's edge,
with here and there an exposure of red granite. It is a
very beautiful stream, and it was a pleasure to get out of
the great river and its oppressive vastness into the familiar-
looking, homely water, its eastern rocks and exquisite curves
and bends. Rounding a point, we came upon a camp of

Chipewyans drying fish and making birch-bark canoes, all of them fat, dirty, like ourselves, and happy; and, passing on, at dusk we reached the outlet and the lake.

It was blowing hard, but we decided to cross to the fort, where a light had been run up for our guidance, and which, by vigorous rowing, we reached by midnight.   Here Mr. Laird was waiting to receive us, the other Commissioners having departed for Fort McMurray and Wahpoóskow.

Next morning we saw the lake to better advantage.   It is called by the Chipewyans Kaytaylaytooway, namely, " The Lake of the Marsh," corresponding to the Athapuskow of the Crees, corrupted into the Rabasca of the French voyageurs, and meaning " The Lake of the Reeds."   At one time, it may be mentioned, it was also known as " The Lake of the Hills," and its great tributary, the Athabasca, was the Elk River; but these names have not survived.

CHAPTER VIII.

FORT CHIPEWYAN TO FORT M'MURRAY.

CHIPEWYAN, it may be remarked, is not a Déné word. It is the name which was given by the Crees to that branch of the race when they first came in contact with them, owing to their wearing a peculiar coat, or tunic, which was pointed both before and behind; now disused by them, but still worn by the Esquimaux, and, until recent years, by the Yukon Indians. Though somewhat similar in sound, it has no connection, it is asserted, with the word Chippeway, or Ojibway. For all that, the words are perhaps closely akin. The writer for the accurate use in this narrative of words in the Cree tongue is under obligation to experts. When preparing his notes to his drama of "Tecumseh" he was indebted to his friend, Mr. Thomas McKay, of Prince Albert, Sask., a master of the Cree language, for the exact origin and derivation of the words Chippeway and Ojibway. Both are corruptions of O-cheepo-way, *cheepo* meaning "tapering," and *way* "sound," or "voice." The name was begot of the Ojibway's peculiar manner of lowering the voice at the end of a sentence. As *"wyan"* means a skin, it is not improbable that the word Chipewyan means tapering or "pointed" skin, referring, of course, to the peculiar garb of the Athapuskow Indians when the Crees first met with them.

The sites of old posts are to be found all over this region; but Chipewyan in the beginning of the last century was the great supply and trading-post of the North-West Company. From Sir John Franklin's Journal (1820) it would appear that the Hudson's Bay Company had begun, and, for some reason not given, had ceased trading on Lake Athabasca, as he says "Fort Wedderburne was a small post built

on Coal Island—now called Potato Island—about A.D.
1815, when the Hudson's Bay Company recommenced trading in this part of the country." He often visited this
island post, then in charge of a Mr. Robertson, and, in June,
engaged there for his memorable journey his bowmen, steers-
men and middlemen, and an interpreter, his other men being
furnished by the rival company. Fort Chipewyan was in
charge at that time of Messrs. Keith and Black, of the North-
West Company, a noticeable feature of the post being a
tower built, Franklin says, about the year 1812, "to watch
Indians who had evil designs."

The site was well chosen, being sheltered from storms from
the lake side by a great bulwark of wooded and rocky
islands. The largest is Potato Island, just opposite, its outliers being the Calf and English Islands—the Lapeta,
Echeranaway and Theyaodene of the Chipewyans; the
Petac, Moostoos and Akayasoo of the Crees.

Fort Chipewyan stands upon a rising ground fronting a
sort of bay formed by these islands, and at the time of our
visit consisted of a trading-store, several large warehouses
and the master's residence, etc., all of solid timber, erected
in the days of Chief-factor MacFarlane, who ruled here
for many years.*

*Mr. MacFarlane's career in the service of the Hudson's Bay Com-
pany is typical of the varied life and movements of its old-time
adventurous traders. He entered the service in 1852, his first winter
being spent as a clerk at Pembina (now Emerson), and also as
trader in charge at the Long Creek outpost. From here he was
transferred to Fort Rae, and afterwards to Fort Good Hope, Mackenzie River, where he remained six years. His next post was Fort
Anderson, on the Begh-ula, or Anderson River, in the Barren
Grounds, which he held for five years, much of his scientific work
being done during excursions from this point. Afterwards he
became trader and accountant at Fort Simpson, and was for two
years in charge of the Mackenzie River district. This was succeeded
by a six months' residence at Fort Chipewyan, where, subsequently,
for fifteen years he had charge of the district. For two years he had
control of the Caledonia district, in British Columbia, but removed
to Fort Cumberland, Sask., where he remained for five years. Other
removals followed until he finally retired from the service, and,
returning to Winnipeg, has lived there ever since.

Inside Fort Chipewyan

Bishop Grouard's Mission and Church at Fort Chipewyan

Colin Fraser's trading-post at Fort Chipewyan

But old as the fort is, it has no relics—not even a venerable cabin. In the store were a couple of not very ancient flint-locks, and, upstairs, rummaging through some dusty shelves, I came across one volume of the Edinburgh, or second, edition of Burns in gray paper boards—a terrible temptation, which was nobly resisted. Though there was once a valuable library here, with many books now rare and costly, yet all had disappeared.

East of the fort are shelving masses of red granite, completely covered by a dark orange lichen, which gives them an added warmth and richness; and on the highest part stood a square lead sun-dial, which, at first sight, I thought had surely been set up by Franklin or Richardson, but which I was told was very modern indeed, and put up, if I am not mistaken, by Mr. Ogilvie, D.L.S. To the west of the fort is the Church of England Mission, and, farther up, the Roman Catholic establishment, the headquarters of our esteemed fellow-voyager, Bishop Grouard.* In line with the fort buildings, and facing the lake, stood a row of whitewashed cottages, all giving the place, with its environs, deeply indented shore and rugged spits of red granite, the

*The first Roman Catholic Mission in Athabasca was formed by Bishop Farrand the year after Bishop Taché's visit to Fort Chipewyan, about A.D. 1849, he being then a missionary priest. Bishop Farrand established other missions on Peace River, and went as far north as Fort Resolution, on Great Slave Lake. He died in 1890, and was succeeded by our guest, Bishop Grouard, O.M.I., *Eveque d'Ibora,* the present occupant of the See of Athabasca and Mackenzie River. This prelate was born at Le Mans, in France, and was educated there, but finished his education in Quebec. He was ordained by Bishop Taché, near Montreal, in 1862, and was sent at once to Chipewyan, where he learnt the difficult language of the natives in a year. He has worked at many points, and perhaps no man in all the North, with the exception of Archdeacon Macdonald, or the late Anglican Bishop Bompas, has or had as accurate a knowledge of the great Déné race, with its numerous subdivisions of Chipewyans, Beavers, Yellow Knives, Dog Ribs, Slaves, Nahanies, Rabbit Skins, Loucheaux, or Squint Eyes (so named from the prevalence of strabismus amongst them), and of other tribes. All these were at one time not only at war with the Crees, but with each other, with the exception of the Slaves, who were always a tame and meek-spirited race, and were often subjected to and treated like dogs by the others. Indeed they were called by the Crees, Awughkanuk, meaning " cattle."

quaint appearance of some secluded fishing village on the
Gulf of St. Lawrence.

In sight, but above the bay, was the trading-post of Colin
Fraser, whose father, the McCrimmon of the North-West,
was Sir George Simpson's piper. The late Chief-factor
Camsell, of Fort Simpson, and myself paddled up to it, and
were most hospitably entertained by Mr. Fraser and his
agreeable family. His father's bagpipes, still in excellent
order, were speedily brought out, and it was interesting to
handle them, for they had heralded the approach of the
autocratic little Governor to many an inland post from
Hudson's Bay to Fraser River, over seventy years before.

Several days were spent at the fort taking declarations,
but, unlike Vermilion or Dunvegan, there were few large
families here, the applicants being mainly young people.
The agricultural resources of this region of rocks are certainly meagre compared with those of Peace River. Potatoes,
where there is any available soil, grow to a good size; barley
was nearly ripe when we were there, and wheat ripens, too.
But, of course, it is not a farming region, nor are fish plentiful at the west end of the lake, the Athabasca River, which
enters there, giving for over twenty miles eastward a muddy
hue to the water. The rest of the lake is crystal clear, and
whitefish are plentiful, also lake trout, which are caught
up to thirty, and even forty, pounds' weight.

The distance from Fort Chipewyan to Fond du Lac is
about 185 miles, but the lake extends over 75 miles farther
eastward in a narrow arm, giving a total length of about 300
miles, the greatest width being about 50 miles. The whole
eastern portion of the lake is a desolate scene of primitive rock and scrub pine, with many quartz exposures,
which are probably mineralized, but with no land, not
even for a garden. The scenery, however, from Black
Bay to Fond du Lac is very beautiful, consisting largely
of islands as diversified and as numerous as the Thousand Islands in the St. Lawrence. These extremely

solitary spots should be, one would think, the breeding-grounds of the pelican, though it is said this bird really breeds on islands in the Great Slave River. If disturbed by man it is reputed to destroy its young and desert the place at once.

The Barren Ground reindeer migrate to the east end of this lake in October, and return in March or April, but this is not certain. Sometimes they unaccountably forsake their old migratory routes, causing great suffering, in consequence, to the Indians. Moose frequent the region, too, but are not numerous, whilst land game, such as prairie chickens, ptarmigan, and a grouse resembling the " fool-hen," is rather plentiful.

The Indians of Fond du Lac are healthy, though somewhat uncleanly in their habits, and fond of dress, which is that of the white man, their women being particularly well dressed.

As an agricultural country the region has no value whatever; but its mineral resources, when developed, may prove to be rich and profitable. Mining projects were already afoot in the country, but far to the north on Great Slave Lake.

What was known as the " Helpman Party " was formed in England by Captain Alene, who died of pneumonia in December, 1898, three days after his arrival at Edmonton. The party consisted of a number of retired army officers, including Viscount Avonmore, with a considerable capital, $50,000 of which was expended. They brought some of their outfit from England, but completed it at Edmonton, and thence went overland late in the spring. But sleighing being about over, they got to Lesser Slave Lake with great difficulty, and there the party broke up, Mr. Helpman and others returning to England, whilst Messrs. Jeffries and Hall Wright, Captain Hall, and Mr. Simpson went on to Peace River Crossing. From there they descended to Smith's Portage, on the Great Slave River, and wintered at Fort Resolution, on Great Slave Lake.

In the following spring they were joined by Mr. McKinlay, the Hudson's Bay Company's agent at the Portage, and he, accompanied by Messrs. Holroyd and Holt, who had joined the party at Smith's Landing, and by Mr. Simpson, went off on a prospecting tour through the north-east portion of Great Slave Lake, staking, *en route,* a number of claims, some of which were valuable, others worthless. The untruthful statements, however, of one of the party, who represented even the worst of the claims as of fabulous value, brought the whole enterprise into disrepute. The members of the party mentioned returned to England ostensibly to raise capital to develop their claims, but nothing came of it, not because minerals of great value do not exist there, but on account of remoteness and the difficulties of transport.

In 1898 another party was formed in Chicago, called " The Yukon Valley Prospecting and Mining Company," its chief promoters being a Mr. Willis and a Mr. Wollums of that city. The capital stock was put at a quarter of a million dollars, twenty-five thousand dollars being paid up. These organizers interested thirty-three other men in the enterprise, the agreement being that these should go to Dawson at the expense of the stockholders, and locate mining claims there, a half-interest in all of which was to be transferred to the company. These men proceeded to Calgary, and outfitted for Dawson, which they wished to reach by ascending the Peace River. At Calgary they were fortunate in procuring as leader a gentleman of large experience in the North, W. J. McLean, Esq., a retired Chief-factor of the Hudson's Bay Company, who pointed out the difficulties of such a route, and recommended, instead, a possible one *via* Great Slave Lake and the Mackenzie River to Fort Simpson, and thence up the Liard River to the height of land at or near Francis Lake, and so down the Pelly River and on to Dawson.

In February the party, led by him, left Edmonton with 160 ponies, sleds and sleighs, loaded with supplies, and pro-

Lake Athabasca at Chipewyan.   The three islands in the offing

Fort Smith and steamer "Grahame," on Great Slave River

Fort Fond du Lac—East end of Lake Athabasca

"Red River" ox-cart.   Still used on the portage at Fort Smith

ceeded, by an extremely difficult forest trail, to Lesser Slave
Lake. They had no feed for the horses, save what they
drew, and, of course, they reached the lake completely
exhausted. Here, by Mr. McLean's advice, they sold the
horses, and with the proceeds hired local freighters to carry
them and their supplies to Peace River Crossing, where
boats were built in which the party, with the exception of
one of the organizers, Mr. Willis, who had returned in
high dudgeon to Chicago, set out for Great Slave Lake.
Before getting to Fort Resolution, Mr. McLean got private
information from a former servant of his at that post,
which led to an expedition to the north-east end of the lake,
where he made valuable finds of copper and other minerals.
Another trip was made, and additional claims were taken,
and on Mr. McLean's return with a lot of samples of ore,
he, with another prospector, came out, and proceeded to
Chicago. His samples were tested there and in Winnipeg,
and yielded in copper from 11 to 32 per cent.; and the
galena 60 ozs. of silver to the ton. Other minerals, such
as sulphur, coal, asphalt, petroleum, iron and salt were discovered, all of great promise, and his opinion is that when
transport is extended to that region, it will prove to be a
great storehouse of mineral wealth.

The other members of the party had at various times and
places separated, some going here and some there; but all
eventually left the country, and the company died a natural
death. But Mr. McLean is not only a firm believer in the
mineral wealth of the North, but in its resources otherwise.
There are extensive areas of large timber, and the lakes
swarm with fish. The soil on the Liard River is excellent,
and he tells me that not only wheat but Indian corn will
ripen there, as he himself grew both successfully when
in charge of that district.

The mining enterprises referred to fell through, but I
have described them at some length since they are very interesting as being the first attempts at prospecting with a view

to development in those remote regions. Failure, of course, at such a distance from transport and supplies, was inevitable. But some of the prospectors, Captain Hall and others who came out with ourselves, seemed to have no doubt that much of the country they explored is rich in minerals. Indeed, should the ancient repute of the Coppermine River be justified by exploration, perhaps the most extensive lodes on the continent will yet be discovered there.

If the Hudson's Bay route were developed, a short line of rail from the western end of Chesterfield Inlet would tap the mining regions prospected, and develop many great resources at present dormant. The very moss of the Barren Lands may yet prove to be of value, and be shipped to England as a fertilizer. I have been told by a gentleman who has travelled in Alaska that an enterprising American there is preparing to collect and ship moss to Oregon, where it will be fermented and used as a fertilizer in the dairy industry.

To return to Lake Athabasca. It seemed at one time to have been the rallying-place of the great Tiné or Déné race, to which, with the exception of the Crees, the Loucheaux, perhaps, and the Esquimaux, all the Indians of the entire country belong. It is said to have been a traditional and central point, such as Onondaga Lake was to the Iroquois.

It is noticeable that, in the nomenclature of the various Indians of the continent, the names by which they were known amongst themselves generally meant men, " original men," or people; *e.g.,* the Lenni Lenápe of the Delawares, with its equivalent, the Anishinápe of the Saulteaux, and the Naheowuk of the Crees. It is also the meaning of the word Déné, the generic name of a race as widely sundered, if not as widely spread, as the Algonquin itself.

The Chipewyan of Lake Athabasca speaks the same tongue as the Apaché of Arizona, the Navajo of Sonora, the Hoopa of Oregon, and the Sarcee of Alberta. The word Apaché has the same root-meaning as the word Déné, though that fierce race was also called locally the Shisíndins, namely,

"The Forest People," doubtless from its original habitat in this region.

Owing to the agglutinative character of the aboriginal languages, numbering over four hundred, some philologists are inclined to attribute them all to a common origin, the Basque tongue being one of the two or three in Europe which have a like peculiarity. In the languages of the American Indians one syllable is piled upon another, each with a distinct root-significance, so that a single word will often contain the meaning of an ordinary English sentence. This polysynthetic character undoubtedly does point to a common origin, just as the Indo-European tongues trace back to Sanskrit. But whether this is indicative of the ancient unity of the American races, whose languages differed in so many other respects, and whose characteristics were so divergent, is another question.

One interesting impression, begot of our environment, was that we were now emphatically in what might be called "Mackenzie's country." In his "General History of the Fur-Trade," published in London in 1801, Sir Alexander tells us that, after spending five years in Mr. Gregory's office in Montreal, he went to Detroit to trade, and afterwards, in 1785, to the Grand Portage (Fort William).

The first traders, he tells us, had penetrated to the Athabasca, *via* Methy Portage, as early as 1791, and in 1783-4 the merchants of Lower Canada united under the name of The North-West Company, the two Frobishers—Joseph Frobisher had traded on the Churchill River as early as 1775—and Simon McTavish being managers. The Company, he says, "was consolidated in July, 1787," and became very powerful in more ways than one, employing, at the time he wrote, over 1,400 men, including 1,120 canoemen. "It took four years from the time the goods were ordered until the furs were sold;" but, of course, the profits, compared with the capital invested, were very great, until the strife deepened between the Montrealers and the Hudson's Bay Company, whose first inland post

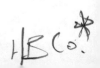

was only established at Sturgeon River, Cumberland Lake, in 1774, by the adventurous, if not over-valiant, Samuel Hearne. The rivalries of these two companies nearly ruined both, until they got rid of them by uniting in 1821, when the Nor'-Westers became as vigorous defenders of King Charles's Charter as they had before been its defiers and defamers.

Fort Chipewyan was established, Mackenzie says, by Mr. Pond, in 1788, the year after his own arrival at the Athabasca, where, by the way, in the fall of 1787, he describes Mr. Pond's garden at his post on that river as being " as fine a kitchen garden as he ever saw in Canada." Fort Chipewyan, however, though not established by Mackenzie, was his headquarters for eight years. From here he set out in June, 1789, on his canoe voyage to the Arctic Ocean, and from here in October, 1792, he started on his voyage up the Peace River on his way to the Pacific coast, which he reached the following year.

In his history he states: " When the white traders first ventured into this country both tribes were numerous, but smallpox destroyed them." And, speaking of the region at large, he, perhaps, throws an incidental side-light upon the Blackfoot question. " Who the original people were," he says, " that were driven from it when conquered by the Kinisteneaux (the Crees) is not now known, as not a single vestige remains of them. The latter and the Chipewyans are the only people that have been known here, and it is evident that the last mentioned consider themselves as strangers, and seldom remain longer than three or four years without visiting their friends and relatives in the Barren Grounds, which they term their native country."*

*It is a reasonable conjecture that these " original people," driven from Athabasca in remote days, were the Blackfeet Indians and their kindred, who possibly had their base at that time, as in subsequent days, at the forks and on both branches of the Saskatchewan. The tradition was authentic in Dr. (afterwards Sir John) Richardson's time. Writing on the Saskatchewan eighty-eight years ago he places the Eascabs, " called by the Crees the Assinipoytuk, or Stone Indians, west of the Crees, between them and the Blackfeet."

Besides Mackenzie's, another name, renowned in the tragic annals of science, is inseparably connected with this region, viz., that of Franklin, who has already been incidentally referred to. Others recur to one, but these two great names are engrained, so to speak, in the North, and cannot be lightly passed over in any descriptive work. The two explorers were friends, or, at any rate, acquaintances; and, before leaving England, Franklin had a long conversation in London with Mackenzie, who died shortly afterwards. The record of his "Journey to the Shores of the Polar Ocean," accompanied by Doctor Richardson and Midshipmen Back and Hood, in the years 1819-20-21 and '22, practically began at York Factory in August of the former year. The rival companies were still at war, and in making the portage at the Grand Rapids of the Saskatchewan, with a party of Hudson's Bay Company traders, "they advanced," he says, "armed, and with great caution." When he returned on the 14th July, 1822, to York, the warring companies had united, and he and his friends were met there by Governor Simpson, Mr. McTavish, and all the united

---

The Assiniboines are an offshoot of the great Sioux, or Dakota, race called by their congeners the Hohas, or "Rebels." They separated from their nation at a remote period owing to a quarrel, so the tradition runs, between children, and which was taken up by their parents. Migrating northward the Eascabs, as the Assiniboines called themselves, were gladly received and welcomed as allies by the Crees, with whom, as Dr. Richardson says, "they attacked and drove to the westward the former inhabitants of the banks of the Saskatchewan." "The nations," he continues, "driven westward by the Eascabs and Crees are termed by the latter Yatchee-thinyoowuc, translated Slave Indians, but properly 'Strangers.'" This word Yatchee is, of course, the Iyaghchi of the Crees in their name for Lesser Slave River and Lake. Richardson describes them as inhabiting the country round Fort Augustus and the foot of the Rockies, and "so numerous now as to be a terror to the Assiniboines themselves." They are divided, he says, into five nations, of whom the Fall Indians, so called from their former residence at Cole's Falls, near the Forks of the Saskatchewan, were the most numerous, consisting of 500 tents, the Piegans of 400, the Blackfeet of 350, the Bloods of 300, and the Sarcees of 150, the latter tribe being a branch of the Chipewyans which, having migrated like their congeners, the Apaches, from the north, joined the Crees as allies, just as the Assiniboines did from the south.

8

partners, after a voyage by water and land of over 5,500 miles. Franklin spent part of the winter at Cumberland post, which had been founded to counteract the rivalry of Montreal. "Before that time," he says, " the natives took their furs to Hudson's Bay, or sold to the French Canadian traders, who," he adds, " visited this part of the country as early as 1697." If so, the credit for the discovery of the Saskatchewan has been wrongly given to the Chevalier, as he was called, a son of Varenne, Sieur de la Varendrye.

Franklin left Cumberland in January, 1820, by dog train for Chipewyan, *via* Fort Carlton and Green Lake. Fort Carlton was the great food supply post, then and long afterwards, of the Hudson's Bay Company, buffalo and wapiti being very abundant. The North-West Company's fort, called La Montee, was three miles beyond Carlton, and harbored seventy French Canadians and sixty women and children, who consumed seven hundred pounds of meat daily, the ration being eight pounds. This post was at that time in charge of Mr. Hallett, a forebear, if I mistake not, of my old friend, William Hallett, leader of the English Plain Hunt, and a distinguished loyalist in the rebellion of 1869.

Franklin and Back left Fort Carlton on the 8th February, and reached Green Lake on the 17th. The North-West Company's post at the lake was managed by Dugald Cameron, and that of the Hudson's Bay Company by a Mr. MacFarlane, and, having been equipped at both posts with carioles, sledges and provisions, they left "under a fusillade from the half-breed women." From the end of the lake they followed for a short distance a small river, then " crossed the woods to Beaver River, and proceeding along it, passed the mouths of two rivers, the latter of which, they were told, was a channel by which the Indians go to Lesser Slave Lake." On the 11th of March they reached Methy Lake—so called from an unwholesome fish of the burbot species found there, only the liver of which is fit to eat—

crossed the Methy portage on the 13th, and, amidst a chaos
of vast ravines and the wildest of scenery, descended the
next day to the Clearwater River. Thence they followed the
Indian trail on the north bank, passing a noted scene, "a
romantic defile of limestone rocks like Gothic ruins," and,
crossing a small stream, found pure sulphur deposited by
springs and smelling very strongly. On the 17th they got to
the junction of the Clearwater with the Athabasca, where
Fort McMurray now stands, and next day reached the Pierre
au Calumet post, in charge of a Mr. Stewart, who had twice
crossed the mountains to the Pacific coast. The place got its
name from a soft stone found there, of which the Indians
made their pipes.

Franklin notes the "sulphurous springs" and "bituminous salt" in this region, also the statement of Mr. Stewart,
who had a good thermometer, "that the lowest temperature
he had ever witnessed in many years, either at the Athabasca or Great Slave Lake, was 45 degrees below zero," a
statement worth recording here.

On the 26th of March the party arrived at Fort Chipewyan,
the distance travelled from Cumberland House being 857
miles. He notes that at the time of his arrival the fort
was very bare of both buffalo and moose meat, owing, it was
said, to the trade rivalry, and that where some eight hundred packs of fur used to be shipped from that point, only
one-half of that number was now sent. Liquor was largely
used by both companies in trade, and scenes of riot and
violence ensued upon the arrival of the Indians at the fort
in spring, and whom he describes otherwise as "reserved
and selfish, unhospitable and beggars, but honest and affec-
tionate to children." They painted round the eyes, the
cheek-bones and the forehead, and all the race, except the
Dog Ribs and the Beavers, believed that their forefathers
came from the East. The Northern Indians, Franklin says,
suppose that they originally sprang from a dog, and about
A.D. 1815 they destroyed all their dogs, and compelled their

women to take their place. Their chiefs seemed to have
no power save over their own families, and their con-
jurers were supported by voluntary contributions of provisions. These are some of the chief characteristics Franklin
notes of the Indians who frequented Fort Chipewyan, at
which point he spent several months. One extraordinary
circumstance, however, remains to be mentioned. It is that
of a young Chipewyan who lost his wife in her first preg-
nancy. He applied the child to his left breast, from which
a flow of milk took place. " The breast," he adds, " became
of an unusual size." Here he and Back, afterwards
Admiral Back, were joined by Dr. Richardson and Mr.
Hood, who had come from Cumberland House by the difficult Churchill River route, and on July 18th, at noon, the
whole party left the fort on their tragic expedition, the
party, aside from those named, consisting of John Hepburn,
seaman, an interpreter and fifteen voyageurs, including,
unfortunately, an Iroquois Indian, called Michel Teroa-
hante. At two p.m. they entered Great Slave River, here
three-quarters of a mile wide, and, passing Red Deer Islands
and Dog River, encountered the rapids, overcome by seven
or eight portages, from the Casette to the Portage of the
Drowned, all varying in length from seventy to eight
hundred yards.

On the 21st they landed at the mouth of Salt River to
lay in a supply of salt for their journey, the deposits lying
twenty-two miles up by stream. These natural pans, or salt
plains, he describes—and the description answers for to-day
—as " bounded on the north and west by a ridge between
six and seven hundred feet high. Several salt springs issue
at its foot, and spread over the plain, which is of tenacious
clay, and, evaporating in summer, crystallize in the form
of cubes. The poisson inconnu, a species of salmon which
ascends from the Arctic Ocean, is not found, he says, above
this stream. A few miles below it, however, a buffalo
plunged into the river before them, which they killed, and
those animals still frequent the region.

On the 25th of July they passed through the channel
of the Scaffold to Great Slave Lake, and, landing at Moose
Deer Island, found thereon the rival forts, of course, within
striking distance of each other, and in charge, as usual, of
rival Scotsmen.   At Great Slave Lake I must part company with Franklin's Journal, since our own negotiations
only extended to its south shores.   But who that has read
it can ever forget the awful return journey of the party
from the Arctic coast, through the Barren Lands, to their
own winter quarters, which they so aptly named Fort Resolution ?   In the tales of human suffering from hunger there
are few more terrible than this.   All the gruesome features
of prolonged starvation were present; the murder of Mr.
Hood and two of the voyageurs by the Iroquois; his bringing to the camp a portion of human flesh, which he declared
to be that of a wolf; his death at the Doctor's hands; the
dog-like diet of old skins, bones, leather pants, moccasins,
tripe de roche; the death of Peltier and Semandre from
want, and the final relief of the party by Akaitcho's Indians,
and their admirable conduct.   And all those horrors experienced over five hundred miles beyond Fort Chipewyan,
itself thousands of miles beyond civilization!   Did the
noble Franklin's last sufferings exceed even these ?   Perhaps;
but they are unrecorded.
   To return to our muttons.   Some marked changes had
taken place, and for the better, in Chipewyan characteristics since Franklin's day; not surprising, indeed, after
eighty years of contact with educated, or reputable, white
men; for miscreants, like the old American frontiersmen,
were not known in the country, and if they had been,
would soon have been run out.   There was now no paint
or " strouds " to be seen, and the blanket was confined to
the bed.   In fact, the Indians and half-breeds of Athabasca Lake did not seem to differ in any way from those
of the Middle and Upper Peace River, save that the former were all hunters and fishermen, pure and simple, there
being little or no agriculture.   It was impossible to study

the manners and customs of the aborigines, since we had
no time to observe them closely. They have their legends
and traditions and remnants of ceremonies, much of which
is upon record, and they cherish, especially, some very
curious beliefs. One, in particular, we were told, obtained
amongst them, namely, that the mastodon still exists in the
fastnesses of the Upper Mackenzie. They describe it as a
monster many times larger than the buffalo, and they dread
going into the parts it is supposed to haunt. This singular
opinion may be the survival of a very old tradition regarding that animal, but is more likely due to the presence of
its remains in the shape of tusks and bones found here and
there throughout the Mackenzie River district and the
Yukon.*

On the 9th the steamer *Grahame* arrived from Smith's
Landing, bringing with her about 120 baffled Klondikers,
returning to the United States, there being still some sixty
more, they said, down the Mackenzie River, who intended
to make their way out, if possible, before winter. They
had a solitary woman with them who had discarded a duffer
husband, and who looked very self-reliant, indeed, being
girt about with bowie-knife and revolver, but otherwise not
alarming.

---

*A similar belief, it is said, exists amongst the Indians of the
Yukon. The remains of the primeval elephant are exceedingly
abundant in the tundras of Siberia, and a considerable trade in
mammoth ivory has been carried on between that region and England for many years. It is supposed that the Asian elephant
advanced far to the North during the interglacial period and
perished in the recurrent glacial epoch. Its American congener,
the mastodon, found its way from Asia to this continent during the
Drift period, when, it is believed, land communication existed in
what is now Bering's Strait, and perished in a like manner. It
was not a sudden but a gradual extinction in their native habitats,
due to natural causes, such as encroaching ice and other material
changes in the animals' environment. This, I believe, is the accepted
scientific opinion of to-day. But the fact that these animals are
at times exposed entire by the falling away of ice-cliffs or ledges,
their flesh being quite fresh and fit food for dogs, and even men,
opens up a very interesting field of inquiry and conjecture. In the
bowels of a mammoth recently revealed in North-Eastern Siberia

It was certainly a motley crowd, and some of its members by no means honest. Chief-factor Camsell, who had just come from Fort Simpson, told me they had stolen from every house where they had a chance, and mentioned, amongst other things, a particularly ungrateful theft of a whip-saw from a native's cabin shortly after an Indian had, with much pains, overtaken them with a similar one, which they had lost on the trail. Their departure, therefore, was not lamented, and the natives were glad to get rid of them.

We ourselves boarded the steamer for Fort McMurray on the 11th, but, owing to bad weather, did not get off till midday, and even then the lake was so rough that we had to anchor for a while in the lee of an island. Colin Fraser had started ahead of us with his big scow and cargo of furs, valued at $15,000, and kept ahead with his fine crew of ten expert trackers. When the weather calmed we steamed across to the entrance of one of the various channels connecting the Athabasca River with the lake, and soon found ourselves skirting the most extensive marshes and feeding-grounds for game in all Canada; a delta renowned throughout

vegetable food was found, probably tropical, at all events unknown to the botany of to-day. The foregoing facts seem to be at variance with the doctrine of Uniformity, or with anything like a slow process. The entombment of these animals must have been very sudden, and due, one would naturally think, to a tremendous cataclysm followed by immediate freezing, else their flesh would have become tainted. A recent English writer predicts another deluge owing to the constant accumulation of ice at the Antarctic Pole, which for untold ages has been attracting and freezing the waters of the Northern Hemisphere. A lowering process, he says, has thus been going on in the ocean levels to the north through immeasurable time, its record being the ancient water-marks now high up on the mountain sides of British Columbia and elsewhere. It is certainly not unthinkable that, if subject to such a displacement of its centre of gravity, our planet at some inconceivably remote period capsized, so that what were before the Tropics became the Poles, and that such a catastrophe is not only possible but is certain to happen again. As a conjecture it may be unscientific; but how many of the accepted theories of science have ceased to be! As a matter of fact, she has been very busy burying her dead, particularly of late years, and her theory of the extinction of the primeval elephant may yet prove to be one of them.

Scientific conjecture

"strange Manuscript found in a copper cylinder."

the North for its abundance of waterfowl, far surpassing the St. Clair flats, or any other region in the East.

Next morning, upon rounding a point, three full-grown moose were seen ahead, swimming across the river. An exciting, and even hazardous, scene ensued on board, the whole Klondike crowd firing, almost at random, hundreds of shots without effect. Two of the noble brutes kept on, and reached the shore, disappearing in the woods; but the third, a three-year-old bull moose, foolishly turned, and lost its life in consequence. It was hauled on deck, bled and flayed, and was a welcome addition to the steamer's table.

That night a concert was improvised on deck, in which the music-hall element came to the front. But one speedily tired of the "Banks of the Wabash," and other ditties; in fact, we were burning to get to Fort McMurray, where we expected letters and papers from the outer world and home, and nothing else could satisfy us. By evening we had passed Burnt Point, also Poplar Point, where the body of an unfortunate, called Patterson, who had been drowned in one of the rapids above, was recovered in spring by some Indians, the body being completely enclosed in a transparent coffin of ice. On the following day we passed Little Red River, and next morning reached the fort, where, to our infinite joy, we received the longed-for letters and papers—our first correspondence from the far East.

Fort McMurray consisted of a tumble-down cabin and trading-store on the top of a high and steep bank, which had yet been flooded at times, the people seeking shelter on an immense hill which overlooked it. Above an island close by is the discharge of the Clearwater River, the old canoe route by which the supplies for the district used to come, via Isle a la Crosse. At McMurray we left the steamer and took to our own boats, our Commission occupying one, and Mr. Laird and party the other. The trackers got into harness at once, and made very good time for some miles, the current not being too swift just here for fast travelling.

The bull moose killed in the Athabasca below Fort McMurray

The Half-breed Commission Boat leaving Fort McMurray to ascend the Athabasca. Pierre Cyr at the bow

Bank of the Athabasca above Fort McMurray

CHAPTER IX.

THE ATHABASCA RIVER REGION.

WE were now traversing perhaps the most interesting
region in all the North. In the neighbourhood of McMurray
there are several tar-wells, so called, and there, if a hole is
scraped in the bank, it slowly fills in with tar mingled with
sand. This is separated by boiling, and is used, in its native
state, for gumming canoes and boats. Farther up are
immense towering banks, the tar oozing at every pore, and
underlaid by great overlapping dykes of disintegrated limestone, alternating with lofty clay exposures, crowned with
poplar, spruce and pine. On the 15th we were still following the right bank, and, anon, past giant clay escarpments
along it, everywhere streaked with oozing tar, and smelling
like an old ship.

These tar cliffs are here hundreds of feet high, of a bold
and impressive grandeur, and crowned with firs which
seem dwarfed to the passer-by. The impregnated clay
appears to be constantly falling off the almost sheer face of
the slate-brown cliffs, in great sheets, which plunge into
the river's edge in broken masses. The opposite river bank
is much more depressed, and is clothed with dense forest.

The tar, whatever it may be otherwise, is a fuel, and
burned in our camp-fires like coal. That this region is
stored with a substance of great economic value is beyond
all doubt, and, when the hour of development comes, it will,
I believe, prove to be one of the wonders of Northern
Canada. We were all deeply impressed by this scene of
Nature's chemistry, and realized what a vast storehouse of
not only hidden but exposed resources we possess in this
enormous country. What is unseen can only be conjec-

121

tured; but what is seen would make any region famous.
We now came once more to outcrops of limestone in regular
layers, with disintegrated masses overlying them, or sand-
wiched between their solid courses. A lovely niche, at one
point, was scooped out of the rock, over the coping of which
poured a thin sheet of water, evidently impregnated with
mineral, and staining the rock down which it poured with
variegated tints of bronze, beautified by the morning sun.

With characteristic grandeur the bends of the river
"shouldered" into each other, giving the expanses the
appearance of lakelets; and after a succession of these we
came to the first rapid, "The Mountain"—Watchíkwe
Powistic—so called from a peak at its head, which towered
to a great height above the neighbouring banks. The rapid
extends diagonally across the river in a low cascade, with
a curve inward towards the left shore. It was decided to
unload and make the portage, and a very ticklish one it
was. The boats, of course, had to be hauled up stream by the
trackers, and grasping their line I got safely over, and was
thankful. How the trackers managed to hold on was to me a
mystery; but the steep and slippery bank was mere child's
play to them. The right bank, from its break and downward,
bears a very thick growth of alders, and here we found the
wild onion, and a plant resembling spearmint.

In the evening we reached the next rapid, called the
Cascades—Nepe Kabátekik—"Where the water falls," and
camping there, we had a symposium in our tent, which I
could not enjoy, having headache and heartburn, a nasty
combination. The 16th was the hottest day of the season—
a hard one on the trackers, who now pulled along walls
of solid limestone, perpendicular or stepped, or wrought
into elaborate cornices, as if by the art of some giant stone-
cutter. At one place we came to a lovely little *rideau,* and
on the opposite shore were two curious caves, scooped out
of the rock, and supported by Egyptian-like columns wrought
by the age-action of water.

Towards evening we reached the Crooked Rapid—Kahwa-
kak o Powestik—and here the portage path followed on the
summit of the limestone rampart, which the viscous gumbo-
slides made almost impassable in rainy weather, and indeed
very dangerous, forming, at the time we passed, pits of
mud and broken masses of half-hard clay, along the very
verge of the wall of rock, likely at any moment to give way
and precipitate one into the raging torrent below.   At other
parts the path was jammed out to the wall-edge, to be stepped
round with a gulp in the throat.   But these and other features of a like interesting character, though a lively experience to the tenderfoot, were of no account whatever to those
wonderful trackers.   At one of the worst spots I was hesi-
tating as to how and where I should step next, when a
carrier, returning for his load, seeing my fix, humped his
back with a laugh and gave me a lift over.

We camped for the night below a point where the river
makes a sharp bend, parallel with its course.   This we surmounted in the morning, following a rounded wall of limestone, for all the world like a decayed rampart of some
ancient city.   A wide floor of rock at its base made beautiful walking to a place where the lofty escarpment showed
exposures of limestone underlying an enormous mass of
dark sandstone, topped by tar-clay.   It is a portentous cliff,
bearing a curiously Eastern look, as if some great pyramid
had been riven vertically, and the exposed surface scarred
and scooped by the weather into a multitude of antic hollows, grotesque projections, and unimaginable shapes.   Here,
also, the knives of passers-by had carved numerous auto-
graphs, marring the majestic cliff with their ludicrous
incongruity.   Are we not all sinners in this way?   "John
Jones," cut into a fantastic buttress which would fittingly
adorn a wizard's temple, may be a poor exhibit of human
vanity; but, after all, the real John Jones is more imperish-
able than the rock, which seems scaling, anyway, from the
top, and may, by and by, carry the inscriptions with it.   It

was hard to tear one's self away from such a wonderful structure as this, the most striking feature of its kind on the whole river.

Farther on, escarped banks, consisting of boulders and pebbles imbedded in tenacious clay, rose to a great height, their tops clothed with rich moss, and wooded with a close growth of pine, the hollows being full of delicious raspberries, now dead ripe.

By and by we encountered the Long Rapids—Kaúkinwauk Powestik—and, some hours afterwards, entered the Middle Rapid—Tuwáo Powestik—the worst we had yet come to, full of boulders and sharp rocks, with a strong current. Very dexterous management was required here on the part of steersman and bowman; a snapt line or a moment's neglect, and a swing to broadside would have followed, and spelled ruin.

It was evening before this rapid was surmounted, and all hands, dog-tired with the long day's pull, were glad to camp at the foot of the Boiler Rapid, the next in our ascent, and so called from the wrecking of a scow containing a boiler for one of the Hudson's Bay Company's steamers. It was the most uncomfortable of camps, the night being close, and filled with the small and bloodthirsty Athabasca mosquito, by all odds the most vicious of its kind. This rapid is strewn with boulders which show above water, making it a very "nice" and toilsome thing to steer and track a boat safely over it, but the tracking path itself is stony and firm, a fortunate thing at such a place. There are no exposures of rock at the foot of this rapid; but along its upper part runs a ledge of asphalt-like rock as smooth as a street pavement, with an outer edge as neatly rounded as if done with a chisel. This was the finest bit of tracking path on the river, excepting, perhaps, the great pavement beneath the cliff at the Long Rapids.

In this region the river scenery changes to a succession of cut-banks, exposed in all directions, and in almost all

Tracking up an Athabasca rapid

A rest near Grand Rapids

In the Grand Rapids of the Athabasca

situations.   Immense towering hills of sand, or clay, are
cut down vertically, some facing the river, others at right
angles to it, and others inland, and almost inclosed by projecting shoulders of the wooded heights.   These cut-banks
carry layers of stone here and there, and are specked with
boulders, and in some places massed into projecting crests,
which threaten destruction to the passer-by.   Otherwise the
scenery is desolate, mountainous always, and wooded, but
with much burnt timber, which gives a dreary look to the
region.   The cut-banks are unique, however, and would
make the fortune of an Eastern river, though here little
noticed on account of their number.

It was now the 18th, and the weather was intensely hot,
foreboding change and the August freshet. We had camped
about eight miles below the Burnt Rapid, and the men were
very tired, having been in the water pretty much since morning.   Directly opposite our camp was a colossal cliff of clay,
around which, looking upward, the river bent sharply to the
south-west, very striking as seen beneath an almost full
moon breaking from a pile of snowy clouds, whilst dark
and threatening masses gathered to the north.   The early,
foggy morning revealed the freshet.   The river, which had
risen during the night, and had forced the trackers from
their beds to higher ground, was littered from bank to bank
with floating trees, logs and stumps, lifted from many a
drift up stream, and borne down by the furious current.   At
one of the short breathing spells the water rose two inches
in twenty minutes, and the tracking became exceedingly bad,
the men floundering to their waists in water, or footing it
insecurely on steep and slippery ledges along the water's
marge.   About mid-day the anticipated change took place
in the weather.   Thick clouds closed in with a driving rain
and a high raw wind, presaging the end of summer.

It was now, of course, very bad going, and camp was made,
in the heavy rain, on a high flat about two miles below the
Burnt Rapid.   Though a tough spot to get up to, the flat

proved to be a prime place for our camp, with plenty of dead fallen and standing timber, and soon four or five "long fires" were blazing, a substantial supper discussed, and comfort succeeded misery. The next day (Sunday) was much enjoyed as a day of rest, the half-breeds at their beloved games, the officials writing letters. The weather was variable; the clouds broke and gathered by turns, with slight rain towards evening, and then it cleared. As a night camp it was picturesque, the full moon in the south gleaming over the turbid water, and the boatmen lounging around the fires like so many brigands.

Next morning we surmounted the Brulé Rapid—Pusitáo Powestik—short but powerful, with a sharp pointed rock at its head, very troublesome to get around. Above this rapid the bank consists of a solid, vertical rampart of red sandstone, its base and top and every crack and crevice clothed with a rich vegetation—a most beautiful and striking scene, forming a gigantic amphitheatre, concentred by the seeming closing-in of the left bank at Point Brulé upon the long straight line of sandstone wall on the right. Nothing finer, indeed, could be imagined in all this remarkable river's remarkable scenery than this impressive view, not from jutting peaks, for the sky-line of the banks runs parallel with the water, but from the antique grandeur of their sweep and apparent junction.

That afternoon we rounded Point Brulé, a high, bold cliff of sandstone with three "lop-sticks" upon its top. The Indian's lop-stick, called by the Cree piskootenusk, is a sort of living talisman which he connects in some mysterious way with his own fate, and which he will often go many miles out of his direct course to visit. Even white men fall in with the fetish, and one of the three we saw was called "Lambert's lop-stick." I myself had one made for me by Gros Oreilles, the Saulteau Chief, nearly forty years ago, in the forest east of Pointe du Chene, in what is now Manitoba. They are made by stripping a tall spruce tree of a deep ring of branches, leaving the top and bottom ones intact. The tree seems to thrive all the same, and is a very noticeable, and not infrequent, object throughout the whole Thickwood Indian country.

Just opposite the cliff referred to, the Little Buffalo, a swift creek, enters between two bold shoulders of hills, and on its western side are the wonderful gas springs. The " amphitheatre " sweeps around to, and is cloven by, that stream, its elevation on the west side being lofty, and deeply grooved from its summit downward, the whole locality at the time of our visit being covered with raspberry bushes loaded with fruit.

The gas escapes from a hole in the ground near the water's edge in a pillar of flame about thirty inches high, and which has been burning time out of mind. It also bubbles, or, rather, foams up, for several yards in the river, rising at low water even as far out as mid-stream. There is a level plateau at the springs, several acres in extent, backed by a range of hills, and if a stake is driven anywhere into this, and withdrawn, the gas, it is said, follows at once. They are but another unique feature of this astonishing stream.

For a long distance the upper prairie level exposes good soil, always clay loam, and there can be little doubt that there is much fertile land in this district. That night we slept, or tried to sleep, in the boat, and made a very early start on a raw, cloudy morning, the tracking being mainly in the water. We now passed great cliffs of sandstone, some almost shrouded in the woods, and came upon many peculiar circular stones, as large as, and much resembling, mill-stones. Towards evening we passed Pointe la Biche, and met Mr. Connor, a trader, with two loaded York boats, going north, and whom we silently blessed, for he brought additional mail for ourselves. What can equal the delight in the wilderness of hearing from home! It was impossible to make Grand Rapids, and we camped where we were, the night cold and raw, but enlivened by the reading and re-reading of letters and newspapers.

Next morning, crossing the right bank of the river, and leaving the boat, we walked to the foot of Grand Rapids. Our path, if it could be called such, lay over a toilsome jumble of huge, sharp-edged rocks, overhung by a beetling cliff of reddish-yellow sandstone, much of which seemed on the point of falling. This whole bank, like so much of this part of the river, is planted, almost at regular intervals, with the great circular rocks already referred to. These globular or circular masses are a curious feature of this region. They have been shaped, no doubt, by the action of eddying water, yet are so numerous, and so much alike, as to bespeak some abnormally uniform conditions in the past.

The Grand Rapids—Kitchi Powestik—the most formidable on the river, are divided by a narrow, wooded island, over a quarter of a mile in length, upon which the Hudson's Bay Company have a wooden tramway, the cars being pushed along by hand. Towards the foot of the island is a smaller one near the left shore, and here is the larger cascade, a very violent rapid, with a fall from the crest to the foot of the island of thirty feet, more or less. The narrower passage is to the right of the island, and is called the " Free Traders' Channel." The river, in full freshet, was very muddy-looking, detracting much from the beauty of the rapids.

The Hudson's Bay Company have storehouses at each end of the tramway, but for their own use only. Free-traders have to portage their supplies over a very rough path beneath the cliffs. Both banks of the river are of sandstone, capped on the left by a wall of cream-coloured rock, seventy or eighty feet in height, at a guess. A creek comes in from the west which has cloven the sandstone bank almost to the water's edge; and running along the top of these sandstone formations are, everywhere, thick layers of coal, which is also found, in a great bed, on the opposite shore, and about three miles back from the river. The coal had been used by a trapper there, and is a good burner and heater, leaving

View on the Athabasca near the Landing

Tracking past grotesque alto-relievos on an Athabasca cut-bank

Tracking up the Grand Rapids of the Athabasca—The Island and
H. B. Co. storehouse in the background

little ash or clinker. These coal beds seem to extend in all directions, on both sides of the river, and underlie a very large extent of country. The inland country for some eight or ten miles had been examined by Sergeant Anderson, of the Mounted Police post here, who described it as consisting of wide ridges, or tables, of first-rate soil, divided by shallow muskegs; a good farming locality, with abundance of large, merchantable spruce timber. Moose were plentiful in the region, and it was a capital one for marten, one white trapper, the winter before our visit, having secured over a hundred skins.

On the 25th we left our comfortable spruce beds and " long fires," and tracked on to House River, which we reached at nine a.m. Here there is a low-lying, desolate-looking, but memorable, " Point," neighboured by a concave sweep of bank. The House is a small tributary from the east, but very long, rising far inland; and here begins the pack-trail to Fort McMurray, about one hundred miles in length, and which might easily be converted into a waggon-road, as also another which runs to Lac la Biche. Both trails run through a good farming country, and the former waggon-road would avoid all the dangers and laborious rapids whose wearisome ascent has been described.

The Point itself is tragic ground, showing now but a few deserted cabins and some Indian graves—one of which had a white paling around it, the others being covered with gray cotton—which looked like little tents in the distance. These were the graves of an Indian and his wife and four children, who had pitched through from Lac la Biche to hunt, and who all died together of diphtheria in this lonely spot. But here, too, many years ago, a priest was murdered and eaten by a weeghteko, an Iroquois from Caughnawaga. The lunatic afterwards took an Indian girl into the depths of the forest, and, after cohabiting with her for some time, killed and devoured her. Upon the fact becoming known, and being pursued by her tribe, he fled to the scene of his

9

horrible banquet, and there took his own life. Having
rowed across the river for better tracking, as we crawled
painfully along, the melancholy Point with its lonely graves,
deserted cabins and cannibal legend receded into eerie distance and wrapped itself once more in congenial solitude.

The men continued tracking until ten a.m., much of the
time wading along banks heavily overhung with alders, or
along high, sheer walls of rock, up to the armpits in the
swift current. The country passed through was one giant
mass of forest, pine and poplar, resting generally upon
loamy clay—a good agricultural country in the main,
similar to many parts of Ontario when a wilderness.

We camped at the Joli Fou Rapids, having only made
about fifteen miles. It was a beautiful spot, a pebbly shore,
with fine open forest behind, evidently a favourite camping-place in winter. Next morning the trackers, having
recrossed for better footing, got into a swale of the worst
kind, which hampered them greatly, as the swift river was
now at its height and covered with gnarled driftwood.

The foliage here and there showed signs of change, some
poplars yellowing already along the immediate banks, and
the familiar scent of autumn was in the air. In a word,
the change so familiar in Manitoba in August had taken
place here, to be followed by a balmy September and the
fine fall weather of the North, said to surpass that of the
East in mildness by day, though perhaps sharper by night.
We were now but a few miles from the last obstruction, the
Pelican Rapids, and pushed on in the morning along banks
of a coal-like blackness, loose and friable, with thin cracks
and fissures running in all directions, the forest behind
being the usual mixture of spruce and poplar. By mid-
day we were at the rapids, by no means formidable, but
with a ticklish place or two, and got to Pelican Portage in
the evening, where were several shanties and a Hudson's
Bay freighting station. Here, too, is a well which was sunk
for petroleum, but which struck gas instead, blowing up

the borer. It was then spouting with a great noise like the blowing-off of steam, and, situated at such a distance from the shaft at the Landing and from the Point Brulé spiracle described, indicated, throughout the district, available resources of light, heat and power so vast as almost to beggar imagining.

Mr. Ross having obtained on the 14th the adhesion of the Crees to the Treaty at Wahpooskow, it was now decided that the Scrip Commission should make the canoe trip to that lake, whilst Mr. Laird and party would go on to Athabasca Landing on their way home. Accordingly Matcheese —" The Teaser "—a noted Indian runner, was dispatched with our letters to the Landing, 120 miles up the river. This Indian, it was said, had once run from the Landing to Edmonton, ninety-five miles, in a single day, and had been known to carry 500 pounds over a portage in one load. I myself saw him shoulder 350 pounds of our outfit and start off with it over a rough path. He was slightly built, and could not have weighed much over nine stone, but was what he looked to be, a bundle of iron muscles and nerves.

On the 29th Mr. Laird and party bade us good-bye, and an hour later we set out on our interesting canoe trip to the Wahpooskow, a journey which led us into the heart of the interior, and proved to be one of the most agreeable of our experiences.

CHAPTER X.

THE TRIP TO WAHPOOSKOW

Our route lay first up the Pelican River, the Chachákew of the Crees, and then from the "divide" down the Wahpooŝkow watershed to the lake. We had six canoemen, and our journey began by "packing" our outfit over a four-mile portage, commencing with a tremendously long and steep hill, and ending on a beautiful bank of the Pelican, a fine brown stream about one hundred feet wide, where we found our canoes awaiting us, capital "Peterboroughs," in good order. Here also were a number of bark canoes, carrying the outfit of Mr. Ladoucere, a half-breed trader going up to Wahpooŝkow. Mr. Prudhomme and myself occupied one canoe, and with two experienced canoemen, Auger. at the stern and Cardinal at the bow, we kept well up with the procession.

Where the channels are shallow, poles are used, which the men handled very dexterously, nicking in and out amongst the rocks and rapids in the neatest way; but in the main the propulsion was by our paddles, a delight to me, having been bred to canoeing from boyhood. We stopped for luncheon at a lovely "place of trees" overhanging a deep, dark, alluring pool, where we knew there were fish, but had no time to make a cast. So far the banks of the Pelican were of a moderate height, and the adjacent country evidently dry—a good soil, and berries very plentiful. Presently, between banks overhung with long grass, birch and alder, we entered a succession of the sweetest little rapids and riffles imaginable, the brown water dancing amongst the

R. N. W. M. Police Post at Grand Rapids of the Athabasca

A typical half breed fireplace and chimney
at Wahpooskow—cabin removed

The lady Klondiker
(See page 118)

stones and boulders to its own music, and the rich rose-pink, cone-like tops of the water-vervain, now in bloom, dancing with it.

Our camp that night was a delightful one, amongst slender birch and spruce and pine, the ground covered with blue-berries, partridge berries, and cranberries in abundance. The berries of the wolf-willow were also red-ripe, alluring, but bitter to the taste. It was really a romantic scene. Ladoucere had made his camp in a small glade opposite our own, the bend of the river being in front of us. The tall pines cast their long reflections on the water, our great fires gleamed athwart them, illuminating the under foliage of the birches with magical light, whilst the half-breeds, grouped around and silhouetted by the fires, formed a unique picture which lingers in the memory. We slept like tops that night beneath the stars, on a soft bed of berry bushes, and never woke until a thin morning rain sprinkling in our faces fetched us to our feet.

A good bacon breakfast and then to our paddles, the river-bends as graceful as ever, but with fewer rapids. At every turn we came upon luxuriant hay meadows, with generally heavy woods opposite them, the river showing the same easy and accessible shore, whilst now and then giant hoof-prints, a broken marge, and miry grass showed where a moose had recently sprawled up the bank. Nothing, indeed, could sur-pass the rich colour-tone of this delightful stream—an exquisite opaqueness even under the clouds; but, interfused with sunshine, like that rare and translucent brown spread by the pencil of a master.

As we were paddling along, the willows on shore suddenly parted, and an Indian runner appeared on the bank, who hailed us and, handing over a sack of mail with letters and papers for us all, sped off as suddenly as he came.

It was now the last day of August, raw and drizzly, and having paddled about ten miles through a like country, we came in sight of the Pelican Mountains to the west, and, later on, to a fork of the river called Muskeg Creek, above which our stream narrowed to about eighteen feet, but still deep and fringed with the same extensive hay meadows, and covered here and there with pond lilies, a few yellow ones still in bloom. By and by we reached Muskeg Portage, nearly a mile in length. The path lay at first through dry muskegs covered with blueberries, Labrador tea, and a dwarfed growth of birch, spruce, tamarac, and jackpine, but presently entered and ended in a fine upland wood, full of pea-vines, vetches and wild rose. This is characteristic of the country, muskegs and areas of rich soil alternating in all directions. The portage completed, we took to our canoes again, the stream of the same width, but very crooked, and still bordered by extensive and exceedingly rich hay meadows, which we were satisfied would yield four or five tons to the acre. Small haystacks were scattered along the route, being put up for ponies which haul supplies in winter from Pelican Landing to Wahpooskow.

The country passed through showed good soil wherever we penetrated the hay margin, with, of course, here and there the customary muskegs. The stream now narrowed into a passage deep but barely wide enough for our canoes, our course lying always through tall and luxuriant hay. At last we reached Pelican Lake, a pretty large sheet of water, about three miles across, the body of the lake extending to the south-west and north-east. We crossed it under sail and, landing at the " three mile portage," found a half-breed there with a cart and ponies, which took our outfit over in a couple of trips to Sandy Lake. A very strong headwind blowing, we camped there for the night.

This lake is the height of land, its waters discharging by the Wahpooskow River, whose northern part, miscalled the Loon, falls into the Peace River below Fort Vermilion. The lake is an almost perfect circle, ten or twelve miles in diameter, the water full of fibrous growths, with patches of green scum afloat all over it. Nevertheless, it abounds in pike, dory, and tullabees, the latter a close congener of the whitefish, but finer in flavour and very fat. Indeed, the best fed dogs we had seen were those summering here. The lake, where we struck it, was literally covered with pin-tail ducks and teal; but it is not a good moose country, and consequently the food supply of the natives is mainly fish.

We descried a few half-breed cabins and clearings on the opposite shore, carved out of the dense forest which girdles the lake, and topographically the country seemed to be of a moderate elevation, and well suited for settlement. The wind having gone down, we crossed the lake on the 2nd of September to what is here called Sandy Creek, a very crooked stream, its thick, sluggish current bordered by willows and encumbered with reeds and flags, and, farther on, made a two-mile portage, where at a very bad landing we were joined by the boats, and presently paddled into a great circular pond, covered with float-weed, a very paradise of ducks, which were here in myriads.

Its continuation, called "The Narrows," now flowed in a troubled channel, crossed in all directions by jutting boulders, full of tortuous snies, to be groped along dexterously with the poles, but dropped at last into better water, ending at a portage, where we dined. This portage led to the farmhouse of a Mr. Houle, a native of Red River, who had left St. Vital fifty-eight years before, and was now settled at a beautiful spot on the right bank of the river, and had horses, cows and other cattle, a garden, and raised wheat and other grain, which he said did well, and was evidently prosperous. After a regale of milk we embarked for the first Wahpooskow lake, which we reached in the afternoon.

This is a fine and comparatively clear sheet of water, much frequented by the natives. The day was beautiful, and with a fair wind and sails up we passed point after point sprinkled with the cabins and tepees of the Indians and half-breeds. It was perfectly charming to sweep up to and past these primitive lodgings, with a spanking breeze, and the dancing

waves seething around our bows. Small patches of potatoes
met the eye at every house, making our mouths water with
expectation, for we had now been a long time without them,
and it is only then that one realizes their value.   In the
far distance we discerned the Roman Catholic Mission
church, the primitive building showing up boldly in the
offing, whilst our canoemen, now nearing their own home,
broke into an Indian chant, and were in high spirits.   They
expected a big feast that night, and so did we! I had been
a bit under the weather, with flagging appetite, but felt again
the grip of healthy hunger.

We were now in close contact with the most innocently
wild, secluded, and apparently happy state of things imaginable—a real Utopia, such as Sir Thomas More dreamt not
of, being actually here, with no trace of abortive politics or
irritating ordinance.   Here was contentment in the savage
wilderness—communion with Nature in all her unstained
purity and beauty.   One thought of the many men of mind
who had moralized on this primitive life, and, tired of
towns, of " the weariness, the fever and the fret " of civilization, had abandoned all and found rest and peace in the
bosom of Mother Nature.

The lake now narrowed into a deep but crooked stream,
fringed, as usual, by tall reeds and rushes and clumps of
flowering water-lilies.   A four-mile paddle brought us to a
long stretch of deep lake, the second Wahpooskow, lined on
the north by a lovely shore, dotted with cabins, the central
tall buildings upon the summit of the rising ground being
those of the English " Church Mission Society," in charge
of the Reverend Charles R. Weaver.   Here we were at last
at the inland end of our journey, at Wahpooskow—this, not
the " Wabiscow " of the maps, being the right spelling and
pronunciation of the word, which means in English " The
Grassy Narrows."

The other Missions of this venerable Society in Athabasca,
it may be mentioned, were at the time as follows: Athabasca

Landing, the residence of Bishop Young; Lesser Slave Lake, White Fish Lake, Smoky River, Spirit River, Fort Vermilion, and Fort Chipewyan, in charge, respectively, of the Reverend Messrs. Holmes, White, Currie, Robinson, Scott, and Warwick. The Roman Catholic Mission, already mentioned, had been established three years before our coming by the Reverend J. B. Giroux, at Stony Point, near the outlet of the first lake, the other Oblat Missions in Athabasca—I do not vouch for my accuracy—being Athabasca Landing, Lesser Slave Lake, the residence of Bishop Clût and clergy and of the Sisters of Providence; White Fish Lake, Smoky River, Dunvegan, and St. John, served, respectively, by Fathers Leferriere, Lesserec, and Letreste; Fort Vermilion by Father Joussard, and Fort Chipewyan by Bishop Grouard and the Grey Nuns.

Mr. Weaver, the missionary at Wahpooskow, is an Englishman, his wife being a Canadian from London, Ontario. By untiring labour he had got his mission into very creditable shape. When it is remembered that everything had to be brought in by bark canoes or dog-train, and that all lumber had to be cut by hand, it seemed to be a monument of industry. Before qualifying himself for missionary work he had studied farming in Ontario, and the results of his knowledge were manifest in his poultry, pigs and cows; in his garden, full of all the most useful vegetables, including Indian corn, and his wheat, which was then in stook, perfectly ripe and untouched by frost. This he fed, of course, to his pigs and poultry, as it could not be ground; but it ripened, he told me, as surely as in Manitoba. Some of the natives roundabout had begun raising stock and doing a little grain growing, and it was pleasant to hear the lowing of cattle and the music of the cow-bells, recalling home and the kindly neighbourhood of husbandry and farm.

The settlement was then some twenty years old, and numbered about sixty souls. The total number of Indians and half-breeds in the locality was unknown, but nearly two hundred Indians received head-money, and all were not paid, and the half-breeds seemed quite as numerous. About a quarter of the whole number of Indians were said to be pagans, and the remainder Protestants and Roman Catholics in fair proportion. In the latter denomination, Father Giroux told me, the proportion of Indians and half-breeds, including those of the first lake, was about equal. The latter, he said, raised potatoes, but little else, and lived like the Indians, by fishing and hunting, especially by the former, as they had to go far now for fur and large game.

The Hudson's Bay Company had built a post near Mr. Weaver's Mission, and there was a free-trader also close by, named Johnston, whose brother, a fine-looking native missionary, assisted at an interesting service we attended in the Mission church, conducted in Cree and English, the voices in the Cree hymns being very soft and sweet. Mr. Ladoucere was also near with his trading-stock, so that business, it was feared, would be overdone. But we issued an unexpectedly large number of scrip certificates here, and the price being run up by competition, a great deal of trade followed.

Wahpooskow is certainly a wonderful region for fish, particularly the whitefish and its cousin-german, the tullabee. They are not got freely in winter in the first lake, but are taken in large numbers in the second, where they throng at that season. But in the fall the take is very great in both lakes, and stages were seen in all directions where the fish are hung up by their tails, very tempting to the hungry dogs, but beyond their reach until the crows attack them. The former keep a watchful eye on this process, and when the crows have eaten off the tails, which they invariably attack first, the dogs seize the fish as they drop. When this performance becomes serious, however, the fish are generally removed to stores.

One night, after an excellent dinner at Mr. Weaver's, that grateful rarity with us, we adjourned to a ball or " break-

Canoeing on the Pelican River

Ascending the Chachakew (Pelican River)

Half-breed family drying whitefish at Wahpooskow Lake

down," given in our honour by the local community. It took place in a building put up by a Mr. George, an English catechist of the Mission; a solid structure of logs of some length, the roof poles being visible above the peeled beams. On one of these five or six candles were alight, fastened to it by simply sticking them into some melted tallow. There were two fiddlers and a crowd of half-breeds, of elders, youths, girls and matrons, the latter squatting on the floor with their babes in moss-bags, dividing the delights of the evening between nursing and dancing, both of which were conducted with the utmost propriety. Indeed, it was interesting to see so many pretty women and well-behaved men brought together in this out-of-the-world place. The dances were the customary reels, and, of course, the Red River Jig. I was sorry, however, to notice a so-called improvement upon this historic dance; that is to say, they doubled the numbers engaged in it, and called it " The Wahpooskow Jig." It seemed a dangerous innovation; and the introduction later on of a cotillon with the usual dreary and mechanical calls filled one with additional forebodings. We almost heard " the first low wash of waves where soon shall flow a human sea." But aside from such newfangled features, there was nothing to criticise. The fiddling was good, and the dancing was good, showing the usual expertness, in which performance the women stooped their shoulders gracefully, and bent their brows modestly upon the floor, whilst the men vied with each other in the admirable and complicated variety of their steps. In fact, it was an evening very agreeably spent, and not the less so from its primitive environment. After joining in a reel of eight, we left the scene with reluctance, the memorable Jig suddenly striking on our ears as we wended our way in the darkness to our camp.

As regards farming land in the region, for a long way inland Mr. Weaver and others described it as of the like good quality as at the Mission, but with much muskeg. It is difficult to estimate the extent of the latter, for, being more noticeable than good land, the tendency is to over-estimate. Its proportion to arable land is generally put at about 50 per cent., which may be over or under the truth, for only actual township or topographic surveys can determine it.

The country drained by the lower river, the Loon, as it is improperly called in our maps, navigable for canoes all the way to where it enters the Peace, was described as an extensive and very uniform plateau, sloping gently to the north. To the south the Pelican Mountains formed a noble background to the view from the Mission, which is indeed charming in all directions.

At the mouth of the river, and facing the Mission, a long point stretches out, dividing the lake into two deep arms, the Mission being situated upon another point around which the lake sweeps to the north. The scene recalls the view from the Hudson's Bay Company's post at Lesser Slave Lake, but excels it in the larger extent of water, broken into by scores of bayous, or pools, bordered by an intensely green water-weed of uniform height, and smooth-topt as a well-clipt lawn. Behind these are hay meadows, a continuation of the long line of them we had passed coming up.

Upon the whole, we considered this an inviting region for any farmer who is not afraid to tackle the forest. But whether a railway would pass this way at first seemed to us doubtful. The head of Lesser Slave Lake lies far to the south-west, and there it is most likely to pass on its way to the Peace. What could be supplied, however, is a waggon-road from Wahpooskow to Athabasca Landing, instead of the present dog-trail, which passes many deep ravines, and makes a long detour by Sandy Lake. Such a road should pass by the east end of the first Wahpooskow Lake, thence to Rock Island Lake, and on by Calling Lake to the Landing, a distance of about one hundred miles. Such a road, whilst saving 125 miles of travel by the present route, would cut down the cost of transport by fully one-half.

Wahpooškow had its superstitions and some doubtful customs. For instance, an Indian called Nepapinase—" A Wandering Bolt of Night-Lightning "—lost his son when Mr. Ross was there taking adhesion to the Treaty, and spread the report that he had brought " bad medicine." Polygamy was practised, and even polyandry was said to exist; but we had no time to verify this gossip, and no right to interfere if we had.

On the 6th, a lovely fall morning, we bade good-bye to Wahpooškow, its primitive people, and its simple but ample pleasures. Autumn was upon us. Foliage, excepting in the deep woods, was changing fast, the hues largely copper and russet; hard body-tints, yet beautiful. There were no maples here, as in the East, to add a glorious crimson to the scene; this was given by shrubs, not by trees. The tints were certainly, in the larger growths, less delicate here than there; the poplar's chrome was darker, the willow's mottled chrome more sere. But there was the exquisite pale canary of the birch, the blood-red and yellow of the wild rose, which glows in both hues, the rich crimson of the red willow, with its foil of ivory berries, and the ruddy copper of the high-bush cranberry. These, with many other of the berry bearers and the wild-flowers, yielded their rich hues; so that the great pigments of autumn, crimson, brown and yellow, were everywhere to be seen, beneath a deep blue sky strewn with snowy clouds.

We were now on the return to Pelican Landing, with but few incidents to note by the way, aside from those already recorded. But having occasion to take a declaration at a cabin on our passage along the first lake, we had an opportunity of visiting a hitherto unobserved stratum of Wahpooškow's society.

The path to the cabin and its tepees led up a steep bank, beaten as hard as nails and as slippery as glass; nevertheless, by clutching the weeds which bordered it, mainly nettles, we got on top at last, where an interesting scene met the eye.

This was a half-breed family, the head of which, a shrivelled old fellow, was busy making a paddle with his crooked knife, the materials of a birch-bark canoe lying beside him—and most beautifully they make the canoe in this region.   His wife was standing close by, a smudged hag of most sinister aspect;   also a son and his wife.   On stages, and on the shrubs around, were strewn nets, ragged blankets, frowsy shawls, and a huddle of other shreds and patches;   and, everywhere else, a horde of hungry dogs snarling and pouncing upon each other like wolves.   Filth here was supreme, and the *mise en scene* characteristic of a very low and very rare type of Wahpoóskow life indeed—a type butted and bounded by the word " fish."   An attempt was made to photograph the group, but the old fellow turned aside, and the old woman hobbled into the recesses of a tepee, where we heard her muttering such execrations in Cree as were possible to that innocent tongue.   The hands of the woman at the cabin door were a miracle of grime and scrofula.   Her sluttish locks, together with two children, hung around her;   one of the latter chewing a muddy carrot up into the leaves, an ungainly little imp;   the other was a girl of singularly beautiful features and of perfect form, her large luminous eyes of richest brown reflecting the sunlight from their depths like mirrors—a little angel clad in dirt.   Why other wild things should be delicately clean, the birds, the fishes she lived on, and she be bred amidst running sores and vermin, was one of the mysteries I pondered over when we took to our canoes. For such a pair of eyes, for those exquisite features, some scraggy denizen of Vanity Fair would have given a king's ransom.   Yet here was a thing of beauty, dropped by a vile freak of Nature into an appalling environment of filth and ignorance;   a creature destined, no doubt, to spring into mature womanhood, and lapse, in time, into a counterpart of the bleared Hecate who mumbled her Cree philippics in the neighbouring wigwam.

On our return trip some detours were made, one of which

was to the habitation of another half-breed family at the foot of Sandy Lake, themselves and everything about them orderly, clean and neat; the very opposites of the curious household we had visited the day before. They had a great kettle of fish on the fire, which we bought, and had our dinner there; being especially pleased to note that their dogs were not starved, but were fat and well handled. At the east side of the lake we were delayed trying to catch ponies to make the portage, failing which we got over otherwise by dark, and camped again on the Pelican River. That night there was a keen frost, and ice formed along shore, but the weather was delightfully crisp and clear, and we reached Pelican Landing on the 9th, finding there our old scow and the trackers, with our friend Cyr in command, and Marchand, our congenial cook, awaiting us.

On the 11th we set off for Athabasca Landing, accompanied by a little fleet of trippers' and traders' canoes, and passed during the day immense banks of shale, the tracking being very bad and the water still high. We noted much good timber standing on heavy soil, and on the 14th passed a curious hump-like hill, cut-faced, with a reddish and yellow cinder-like look, as if it had been calcined by underlying fires. Near it was an exposure of deep coloured ochre, and, farther on, enormous black cut-banks, also suggestive of coal.

The Calling River—" Kitoósepe "—was one of our points of distribution, and upon reaching it we found the river benches covered with tepees, and a crowd of half-breeds from Calling Lake awaiting us. After the declarations and scrip payments were concluded, we took stock of the surroundings, which consisted, so far as numbers went, mainly of dogs. Nearly all of them looked very miserable, and one starveling bitch, with a litter of pups, seemed to live upon air. It was pitiful to see the forlorn brutes so cruelly abused; but it has been the fate of this poor mongrel friend of humanity from the first. The canine gentry fare better than many a man, but the outcasts of the slums and camps feel the stroke of bitter fortune, yet, with prodigious heart, never cease to love the oppressor.

There was an adjunct of the half-breed camp, however, more interesting than the dogs, namely, Marie Rose Gladu, a half-sister of the Catherine Bisson we met at Lesser Slave Lake, but who declared herself to be older than she by five years. From evidence received she proved to be very old, certainly over a hundred, and perhaps the oldest woman in Northern Canada. She was born at Lesser Slave Lake, and remembered the wars of her people with the Blackfeet, and the " dancing " of captured scalps. She remembered the buffalo as plentiful at Calling Lake; that it was then a mixed country, and that their supplies in those old days were brought in by way of Isle a la Cross, Beaver River, and Lac la Biche, as well as by Methy Portage, a statement which I have heard disputed, but which is quite credible for all that. She remembered the old fort at the south-east end of Lesser Slave Lake, and Waupístagwon, "The White Head," as she called him, namely, Mr. Shaw of the famous finger-nail. Her father, whose name was Nekehwapiškun—" My wigwam is white "—was a fur company's Chief, and, in his youth, a noted hunter of Rabisca (Chipewyan), whence he came to Lesser Slave Lake. Her own Cree name, unmusical for a wonder, was Ochenaskuñagan—" Having passed many Birthdays." Her hair was gray and black rather than iron-gray, her eyes sunken but bright, her nose well formed, her mouth unshrunken but rather projecting, her cheeks and brow a mass of wrinkles, and her hands, strange to say, not shrivelled, but soft and delicate as a girl's. The body, however, was nothing but bones and integument; but, unlike her half-sister, she could walk without assistance. After our long talk through an interpreter she readily consented to be photographed with me, and, seating ourselves on the grass together, she grasped my hand and disposed herself in a jaunty way so as to look her very best. Indeed, she must have been a pretty girl in her youth, and, old as she was, had some of the arts of girlhood in her yet.

The persons seated are Marie Rose Gladu (Ochenaskumagan) and the Author

At this point the issue of certificates for scrip practically ended, the total number distributed being 1,843, only 48 of which were for land.

Leaving Calling River before noon, we passed Riviere la Biche towards evening, and camped about four miles above it on the same side of the river. We were not far from the Landing, and therefore near the end of our long and toil-some yet delightful journey. It was pleasant and unex-pected, too, to find our last camp but one amongst the best. The ground was a flat lying against the river, wooded with stately spruce and birch, and perfectly clear of underbrush. It was covered with a plentiful growth of a curious fern-like plant which fell at a touch. The great river flowed in front, and an almost full moon shone divinely across it, and sent shafts of sidelong light into the forest. The huge camp-fires of the trackers and canoemen, the roughly garbed groups around them, the canoes themselves, the whole scene, in fact, recalled some *genre* sketch by our half-forgotten colourist, Jacobi. Our own fire was made at the foot of a giant spruce, and must have been a surprise to that beautiful creature, evidently brimful of life. Indeed, I watched the flames busy at its base with a feeling of pain, for it is difficult not to believe that those grand productions of Nature, highly organized after their kind, have their own sensations, and enjoy life.

The 17th fell on a Sunday, a delicious morning of mist and sunshine and calm, befitting the day. But we were eager for letters from home, and therefore determined to push on. Perhaps it was less desecrating to travel on such a morning than to lie in camp. One felt the penetrating power of Nature more deeply than in the apathy or indolent ease of a Sunday lounge. Still there were those who had to smart for it—the trackers. But the Mecca of the Landing being so near, and its stimulating delights looming largely in the haze of their imagination, they were as eager to go on as ourselves.

10

The left bank of the river now exhibited, for a long distance, a wilderness swept by fire, but covered with " rampikes " and fallen timber.   The other side seemed to have partially escaped destruction.   The tracking was good, and we passed the " Twenty Mile Rock " before dinner, camping about fifteen miles from the Landing.   Next morning we passed through a like burnt country on both sides, giving the region a desolate and forlorn look, which placed it in sinister contrast with the same river to the north.

Farther up, the right bank rose bare to the sky-line with a mere sprinkling of small aspens, indicating what the appearance of the " rampike " country would be if again set ablaze, and converted from a burnt-wood region to a bare one.   The banks revealed a clay soil, in some places mixed with boulders, but evidently there was good land lying back from the river.

In the morning bets were made as to the hour of arrival at the Landing.   Mr. P. said four p.m., the writer five, the Major six, and Mr. C. eight.   At three p.m. we rounded the last point but one, and reached the wharf at six-thirty, the Major taking the pool.

We had now nothing before us but the journey to Edmonton.   At night a couple of dances took place in adjacent boarding-houses, which banished sleep until a great uproar arose, ending in the partisans of one house cleaning out the occupants of the other, thus reducing things to silence.   We knew then that we had returned to earth.   We had dropped, as it were, from another planet, and would soon, too soon, be treading the flinty city streets, and, divorced from Nature, become once more the bond-slaves of civilization.

CONCLUSION.

I HAVE thought it most convenient to the reader to unite with the text, as it passes in description from place to place, what knowledge of the agricultural and other resources of the country was obtainable at the time. The reader is probably weary of description by this time; but, should he make a similar journey, I am convinced he would not weary of the reality. Travellers, however, differ strangely in perception. Some are observers, with imagination to brighten and judgment to weigh, and, if need be, correct, first impressions; whilst others, with vacant eye, or out of harmony with novel and perhaps irksome surroundings, see, or profess to see, nothing. The readiness, for instance, of the Eastern " fling " at Western Canada thirty years ago is still remembered, and it is easy to transfer it to the North.

Those who lament the meagreness of our records of the fur-trade and primitive social life in Ontario, for example, before the advent of the U. E. Loyalists, can find their almost exact counterpart in Athabasca to-day. For what that Province was then, viz., a wilderness, Athabasca is now; and it is safe to predict that what Ontario is to-day Athabasca will become in time. Indeed, Northern Canada is the analogue of Eastern Canada in more likenesses than one.

That the country is great and possessed of almost unique resources is beyond doubt; but that it has serious drawbacks, particularly in its lack of railway connection with the outer world, is also true. And one thing must be borne in mind, namely, that, when the limited areas of prairie within its borders are taken up, the settler must face the forest with the axe.

147

Perhaps he will be none the worse for this. It bred in the pioneers of our old provinces some of the highest qualities: courage, iron endurance, self-denial, homely and upright life, and, above all, for it includes all, true and ennobling patriotism. The survival of such qualities has been manifest in multitudes of their sons, who, remembering the record, have borne themselves manfully wherever they have gone.

But modern conditions are breeding methods new and strange, and keen observers profess to discern in our swift development the decay of certain things essential to our welfare. We seem, they think, to be borrowing from others— for they are not ours by inheritance—their boastful spirit, extravagance, and love of luxury, fatal to any State through the consequent decline of morality. The picture is overdrawn. True womanhood and clean life are still the keynotes of the great majority of Canadian homes.

Yet very striking is the contrast with the old days of household economies, the days of the ox-chain, the sickle, and the leach-tub. All of these, some happily and some unhappily, have been swept away by the besom of Progress. But in any case life was too serious in those days for effeminate luxury, or for aught but proper pride in defending the country, and in work well done. And it is just this stern life which must be lived, sooner or later, not only in the wilds of Athabasca, but in facing everywhere the great problems of race-stability —the spectres of retribution—which are rapidly rising upon the white man's horizon.

For the rest, and granting the manhood, the future of Athabasca is more assured than that of Manitoba seemed to be to the doubters of thirty years ago. In a word, there is fruitful land there, and a bracing climate fit for industrial man, and therefore its settlement is certain. It will take time. Vast forests must be cleared, and not, perhaps, until railways are built will that day dawn upon Athabasca. Yet it will come; and it is well to know that, when it does, there is ample room for the immigrant in the regions described.

The generation is already born, perhaps grown, which will recast a famous journalist's emphatic phrase, and cry, " Go North!" Well, we came thence! Our savage ancestors, peradventure, migrated from the immemorial East, and, in skins and breech-clouts, rocked the cradle of a supreme race in Scandinavian snows. It has travelled far to the enervating South since then; and, to preserve its hardihood and sway on this continent, must be recreated in the high latitudes which gave it birth.

[Handwritten annotations:]

Aryan race

return to origins
to be reborn
true womanhood
clean life.

". . . And this also was one of the dark places of the earth."
Heart of Darkness.

Thames : Congo
Ont : Athabasca

MR. COTE'S POEM.

Sortez de vos tombeaux, peuplades endormies
A l'ombre des grands pins de vos forêts bénies!
Venez, fils de guerriers, qui jadis sous ces bois
Bruliez vos tomahawks, vos armes et vos carquois!
Que sur vos pâles fronts l'auréole immortelle
Pour votre bienfaiteur s'illumine plus belle.
Néophytes, venez en ce jour de bonheur
Proclamer les vertus de l'illustre pasteur,
Qui pour vous ses agneaux, ses brebis les plus chères.
Consacra sa jeunesse et ses années entières.
Venez, fleurs qui brillez au jardin du Bon Dieu.
Répandre les parfums qu'exhale le saint lieu
Sur l'illustre vieillard qui de sa voix bénie
Vous fit épanouir dans l'hôeureuse patrie!
Tendre et vénéré père, apôtre magnanime,
Grand prêtre du Seigneur, votre oeuvre fut sublime.
Des bords du Missouri jusqu'aux glaces du nord,
Voyez, semeur béni, cinquante sillons d'or;
Voyez sur le versant de la montagne sainte
De votre charité l'impérissable empreinte;
Voyez cette légion d'âmes régénérées
Portant par votre main les célestes livrées.
Quoi, muse profane, indigne chalumeau,
Oserais-tu planer sur un thème si haut?
Pour chanter du héros les fêtes jubilaires
Descends de ces hauteurs à demi-séculaires!
Muse prosterne-toi. Hosanna! Hosanna!
Au ciel gloire au Très-Haut. Jube, alleluia!
Hommage sur la terre à l'Oblat de Marie,
Qui dans son cycle d'or brille sur la patrie!

APPENDICES

Treaty No. 8,
Canada, *Statutes*, 63 Victoria, A. 1900,
Sessional Paper No. 14

Order In Council
Ratifying Treaty No. 8,
Canada, *Statutes*, 63 Victoria, A. 1900,
Sessional Paper No. 14

Report of Commissioners
for Treaty No. 8,
Canada, *Statutes*, 63 Victoria, A. 1900,
Sessional Paper No. 14

Editor's Note: The text herein of Treaty 8 (pp. 155–60) is reproduced according to the version printed in the original Mair edition of *Through the Mackenzie Basin* and although it agrees word-for-word (with one exception—the word "the" appears only in the Mair text in the sixth paragraph) with the original Treaty and the text of the Treaty reproduced in Canada, *Statutes*, 63 Victoria, A. 1900, Sessional Paper No. 14, the punctuation and capitalization varies. The Mair version is grammatically preferable, and the idiosyncrasies of that text are reproduced here. The text from the Treaty signings (pp. 160–68), the Order In Council Ratifying Treaty No. 8, and the Report of Commissioners of Treaty No. 8 are from Canada, *Statutes*, 63 Victoria, A. 1900, Sessional Paper No. 14, and are reproduced as written, including an incorrect date for the signing with the Beaver Indians at Dunvegan in the Report of Commissioners and the inconsistent spelling of present-day Wabasca as Wabiscow or Wapiscow.

And the undersigned Cree, Beaver, Chipewyan and
other Indian Chiefs and Headmen on their own behalf and on
behalf of all the Indians whom they represent, DO HEREBY
SOLEMNLY PROMISE and engage to strictly observe this Treaty,
and also to conduct and behave themselves as good and loyal
subjects of Her Majesty the Queen. THEY PROMISE AND ENGAGE
that they will, in all respects, obey and abide by the law;
that they will maintain peace between each other, and between
themselves and other tribes of Indians, and between themselves
and others of Her Majesty's subjects, whether Indians, Half-
breeds, or Whites, this year inhabiting and hereafter to
inhabit any part of the said ceded territory; and that they
will not molest the person or property of such ceded tract,
of any inhabitant
or of any other district or country, or interfere with or
trouble any person passing or travelling through the said
tract, or any part thereof, and that they will assist the
officers of Her Majesty in bringing to justice and punishment
any Indian offending against the stipulations of this Treaty,
or infringing the laws in force in the country so ceded.

IN WITNESS WHEREOF Her Majesty's said Commissioners,
and the Cree Chief and Headman of Lesser Slave Lake and the
adjacent territory HAVE HEREUNTO SET THEIR HANDS at Lesser
Slave Lake, on the twenty-first day of June in the year herein
first above written.

Signed by the parties hereto,
in the presence of the undersigned witnesses, the same
having been first explained to
the Indians by Albert Tate
and Samuel Cunningham, Interpreters.

*Father A. Lacombe
as adviser of the
Commissioners*
Geo Holmes

*David Laird
Treaty Commissioner*

*J. A. J. McKenna
Treaty Commissioner*

*J. H. Ross
Treaty Commissioner*

*Kee noo shay oo   his Chief
mark*

Photograph of the original text from the signing of Treaty No. 8. NAC

TREATY NO. 8

Canada, Statutes,
63 Victoria, A. 1900,
Sessional Paper No. 14

ARTICLES OF A TREATY made and concluded at the several dates mentioned therein, in the year of Our Lord one thousand eight hundred and ninety-nine, between Her Most Gracious Majesty the Queen of Great Britain and Ireland, by Her Commissioners the Honourable David Laird, of Winnipeg, Manitoba, Indian Commissioner for the said Province and the North-West Territories; James Andrew Joseph McKenna, of Ottawa, Ontario, Esquire, and the Honourable James Hamilton Ross, of Regina, in the North-West Territories, on of the one part; and the Cree, Beaver, Chipewyan and other Indians, inhabitants of the territory within the limits hereinafter defined and described, by their Chiefs and Headmen, hereunto subscribed, of the other part:—

WHEREAS, the Indians inhabiting the territory hereinafter defined have, pursuant to notice given by the Honourable Superintendent-General of Indian Affairs in the year 1898, been convened to meet a Commission representing Her Majesty's

Government of the Dominion of Canada at certain places in the said territory in this present year 1899, to deliberate upon certain matters of interest to Her Most Gracious Majesty, of the one part, and the said Indians of the other.

AND WHEREAS, the said Indians have been notified and informed by Her Majesty's said Commission that it is Her desire to open for settlement, immigration, trade, travel, mining, lumbering, and such other purposes as to Her Majesty may seem meet, a tract of country bounded and described as hereinafter mentioned, and to obtain the consent thereto of Her Indian subjects inhabiting the said tract, and to make a treaty, and arrange with them, so that there may be peace and good will between them and Her Majesty's other subjects, and that Her Indian people may know and be assured of what allowances they are to count upon and receive from Her Majesty's bounty and benevolence.

AND WHEREAS, the Indians of the said tract, duly convened in council at the respective points named hereunder, and being requested by Her Majesty's Commissioners to name certain Chiefs and Headmen who should be authorized on their behalf to conduct such negotiations and sign any treaty to be founded thereon, and to become responsible to Her Majesty for the faithful performance by their respective bands of such obligations as shall be assumed by them, the said Indians have therefore acknowledged for that purpose the several Chiefs and Headmen who have subscribed hereto.

AND WHEREAS, the said Commissioners have proceeded to negotiate a treaty with the Cree, Beaver, Chipewyan and other Indians, inhabiting the district hereinafter defined and described, and the same has been agreed upon and concluded by the respective bands at the dates mentioned hereunder, the said Indians DO HEREBY CEDE, RELEASE, SURRENDER AND YIELD UP to the Government of the Dominion of Canada, for Her Majesty the Queen and her successors for ever, all their rights, titles and privileges whatsoever, to the lands included within the following limits, that is to say:—

Commencing at the source of the main branch of the Red Deer River in Alberta, thence due west to the central range of the Rocky Mountains, thence north-westerly along the said range to the point where it intersects the 60th parallel of north latitude, thence east along said parallel to the point where it intersects Hay River, thence north-easterly down said river to the south shore of Great Slave Lake, thence along the said shore north-easterly (and including such rights to the islands in said lakes as the Indians mentioned in the treaty may possess), and thence easterly and north-easterly along the south shores of Christie's Bay and McLeod's Bay to old Fort Reliance, near the mouth of Lockhart's River, thence south-easterly in a straight line to and including Black Lake, thence south-westerly up the stream from Cree Lake, thence including said lake south-westerly along the height of land between the Athabasca and Churchill Rivers, to where it intersects the northern boundary of Treaty Six, and along the said boundary easterly, northerly and south-westerly, to the place of commencement.

AND ALSO, the said Indian rights, titles and privileges whatsoever to all other lands wherever situated, in the North-West Territories, British Columbia, or in any other portion of the Dominion of Canada.

To HAVE AND TO HOLD the same to Her Majesty the Queen and Her successors for ever.

And Her Majesty the Queen HEREBY AGREES with the said Indians that they shall have right to pursue their usual vocations of hunting, trapping and fishing throughout the tract surrendered as heretofore described, subject to such regulations as may from time to time be made by the Government of the country, acting under the authority of Her Majesty, and saving and excepting such tracts as may be required or taken up from time to time for settlement, mining, lumbering, trading or other purposes.

And Her Majesty the Queen hereby agrees and undertakes to lay aside reserves for such bands as desire reserves, the same not to exceed in all one square mile for each family of five for such number of families as may elect to reside on reserves, or in that proportion for larger or smaller families; and for such families or individual Indians as may prefer to live apart from band reserves, Her Majesty undertakes to provide land in severalty to the extent of 160 acres to each Indian, the land to be conveyed with a proviso as to non-alienation without the consent of the Governor-General-in-Council of Canada, the selection of such reserves, and lands in severalty, to be made in the manner following, namely, the Superintendent-General of Indian Affairs shall depute and send a suitable person to determine and set apart such reserves and lands, after consulting with the Indians concerned as to the locality which may be found suitable and open for selection.

Provided, however, that Her Majesty reserves the right to deal with any settlers within the bounds of any lands reserved for any band as She may see fit; and also that the aforesaid reserves of land, or any interest therein, may be sold or otherwise disposed of by Her Majesty's Government, for the use and benefit of the said Indians entitled thereto, with their consent first had and obtained.

It is further agreed between Her Majesty and Her said Indian subjects that such portions of the reserves and lands above indicated as may at any time be required for public works, buildings, railways, or roads of whatsoever nature, may be appropriate for that purpose by Her Majesty's Government of the Dominion of Canada, due compensation being made to the Indians for the value of any improvements thereon, and an equivalent in land, money or other consideration for the area of the reserve so appropriated.

And with a view to show the satisfaction of Her Majesty with the behaviour and good conduct of Her Indians, and in extinguishment of all their past claims, She hereby, through Her Commissioners, agrees to make each Chief a present of thirty-two dollars in cash, to each Headman twenty-two dollars, and to every other Indians of whatever age, of the families represented at the time and place of payment, twelve dollars.

Her Majesty also agrees that next year, and annually afterwards for ever, She will cause to be paid to the said Indians in cash, at suitable places and dates, of which the said Indians shall be duly notified, to each Chief twenty-five dollars, each Headman, not to exceed four to a large Band and two to a small Band, fifteen dollars, and to every other Indians, of whatever age, five dollars, the same, unless there be some exceptional reason, to be paid only to heads of families for those belonging thereto.

FURTHER, Her Majesty agrees that each Chief, after signing the treaty, shall receive a silver medal and a suitable flag, and next year, and every third year thereafter, each Chief and Headman shall received a suitable suit of clothing.

FURTHER, Her Majesty agrees to pay the salaries of such teachers to instruct the children of said Indians as to Her Majesty's Government of Canada may seem advisable.

FURTHER, Her Majesty agrees to supply each Chief of a Band that selects a reserve, for the use of the Band, ten axes, five hand-saws, five augers, one grindstone, and the necessary files and whetstones.

FURTHER, Her Majesty agrees that each band that elects to take a reserve and cultivate the soil, shall, as soon as convenient after such reserve is set aside and settled upon, and the Band has signified its choice and is prepared to break up the soil, receive two hoes, one spade, one scythe and two hay forks for every family so settled, and for every three families one plough and one harrow, and to the Chief, for the use of his Band, two horses or a yoke of oxen, and for each Band potatoes, barley, oats and wheat (if such seed by suited to the locality of the reserve), to plant the land actually broken up, and provisions for one month in the spring for several years while planting such seeds; and to every family one cow, and every Chief one bull, and one mowing machine and one reaper for the use of his Band when it is ready for them; for such families as prefer to raise stock instead of cultivating the soil, every family of five persons, two cows, and every Chief two bulls and two mowing machine when ready for their use, and a like proportion for smaller or larger families. The aforesaid articles, machines and cattle, to be given once for all for the encouragement of agriculture and stock raising; and for such Bands as prefer to continue hunting and fishing, as much ammunition and twine for making nets annually as will amount in value to one dollar per head of the families so engaged in hunting and fishing.

And the undersigned Cree, Beaver, Chipewyan and other Indian Chiefs and Headmen, on their own behalf and on behalf of all the Indians whom they represent, DO HEREBY SOLEMNLY PROMISE and engage to strictly observe this Treaty, and also to conduct and behave themselves as good and loyal subjects of Her Majesty the Queen.

THEY PROMISE AND ENGAGE that they will, in all respects, obey and abide by the law; that they will maintain peace between each other, and between themselves and other tribes of Indians, and between themselves and others of Her Majesty's subjects, whether Indians, half-breeds or whites, this year inhabiting and hereafter to inhabit any part of the said ceded territory; and that they will not molest the person or property of any inhabitant of such ceded tract, or of any other district or country, or interfere with or trouble any person passing or travelling through the said tract or any part thereof, and that they will assist the officers of Her Majesty in bringing to justice and punishment any Indian offending against the stipulations of this Treaty or infringing the law in force in the country so ceded.

SIGNING AT LESSER SLAVE LAKE

IN WITNESS WHEREOF Her Majesty's said Commissioners and the Cree Chief and Headmen of Lesser Slave Lake and adjacent territory, HAVE HEREUNTO SET THEIR HANDS AT Lesser Slave Lake on the twenty-first day of June, in the year herein first above written.

Signed by the parties hereto, in the presence of the undersigned witnesses, the same having been first explained to the Indians by Albert Tate and Samuel Cunningham, Interpreters.

FATHER A. LACOMBE,
GEO. HOLMES,
† E. GROUARD, O.M.I.,
W.G. WHITE,
JAMES WALKER,
J. ARTHUR COTÉ,
A.E. SNYDER, Insp., N.W.M.P.,
H.B. ROUND,
HARRISON S. YOUNG,
J.F. PRUD'HOMME,
J.W. MARTIN,
C. MAIR,
H.A. CONROY,
PIERRE DESCHAMBEAULT,
J.H. PICARD,
RICHARD SECORD,
M. McCAULEY.

DAVID LAIRD, *Treaty Commissioner,*
J.A.J. McKENNA, *Treaty Commissioner,*
J.H. ROSS, *Treaty Commissioner,*
KEE NOO SHAY OO X *Chief,*
    his
    mark
MOOSTOOS X *Headman,*
    his
    mark
FELIX GIROUX X *Headman,*
    his
    mark
WEE CHEE WAY SIS X *Headman,*
    his
    mark
CHARLES NEE SUE TA SIS X *Headman,*
    his
    mark
CAPTAIN X *Headman,* from Sturgeon Lake.
    his
    mark

SIGNING AT PEACE RIVER LANDING

In witness whereof the Chairman of Her Majesty's Commissioners and the Headman of the Indians of Peace River Landing and the adjacent territory, in behalf of himself and the Indians whom he represents, have hereunto set their hands at the said Peace River Landing on the first day of July in the year of our Lord one thousand eight hundred and ninety-nine.

Signed by the parties hereto,
  in the presence of the
  undersigned witnesses, the
  same having been first
  explained to the Indians
  by Father A. Lacombe and
  John Boucher, interpreters.

{

DAVID LAIRD, *Chairman of the Indian Treaty Commissioners,*
his
DUNCAN X TASTAOOSTS, *Headman*
mark *of Crees.*

A. LACOMBE,
† E. GROUARD, O.M.I., Ev. d'Ibora,
GEO. HOLMES,
HENRY MCCORRISTER,
K.F. ANDERSON, Sgt., N.W.M.P.,
PIERRE DESCHAMBEAULT,
H.A. CONROY,
T.A. BRICK,
HARRISON S.YOUNG,
J.W. MARTIN,
DAVID CURRY.

SIGNING AT VERMILLION

In witness whereof the Chairman of Her Majesty's Commissioners and the Chief and Headman of the Beaver and Headman of the Crees and other Indians of Vermillion and the adjacent territory, in behalf of themselves and the Indians whom they represent, have hereunto set their hands at Vermillion on the eighth day of July, in the year of our Lord one thousand eight hundred and ninety-nine.

Signed by the parties hereto, in the presence of the undersigned witnesses, the same having been first explained to the Indians by Father A. Lacombe and John Bourassa, Interpreters.

A. LACOMBE,
† E. GROUARD, O.M.I., Ev. d'Ibora,
MALCOLM SCOTT,
F.D. WILSON, H.B.Co.,
H.A. CONROY,
PIERRE DESCHAMBEAULT,
HARRISON S. YOUNG,
J.W. MARTIN,
A.P. CLARKE,
CHAS. H. STUART WADE,
K.F. ANDERSON, Sgt., N.W.M.P.

DAVID LAIRD, *Chairman of the Indian Treaty Coms.*,
his
AMBROSE X TETE NOIRE, *Chief*
mark *Beaver Indians,*
his
PIERROT X FOURIER, *Headman*
mark *Beaver Indians,*
his
KUIS KUIS KOW CA POOHOO X
Headman Cree Indians. mark

SIGNING AT FOND DU LAC

In witness whereof the Chairman of Her Majesty's Commissioners and the Chief and Headmen of the Chipewyan Indians of Fond du Lac (Lake Athabasca) and the adjacent territory, in behalf of themselves and the Indians whom they represent, have hereunto set their hands at the said Fond du Lac on the twenty-fifth and the twenty-seventh days of July, in the year of our Lord one thousand eight hundred and ninety-nine.

Signed by the parties hereto,
   in the presence of the
   undersigned witnesses,
   the same having been first
   explained to the Indians
   by Pierre Deschambeault,
   Reverend Father Douceur
   and Louis Robillard,
   Interpreters.

DAVID LAIRD, *Chairman of the Indian Treaty Commissioners,*

         his
LAURENT X DZIEDDIN, *Headman,*
        mark

         his
TOUSSAINT X *Headman,*
        mark

(The number accepting treaty being larger than at first expected, a Chief was allowed, who signed the treaty on the 27th July before the same witnesses to signatures of the Commissioner and Headmen on the 25th.)

G. BREYNAT, O.M.I.,
HARRISON S. YOUNG,
PIERRE DESCHAMBEAULT,
WILLIAM HENRY BURKE,
BATHURST F. COOPER,
GERMAIN MERCREDI,
     his
LOUIS X ROBILLARD,
   mark
K.F. ANDERSON, Sgt., N.W.M.P.

       his
MAURICE X PICHE, *Chief of Band.*
      mark
WITNESS, H.S. YOUNG,

SIGNING AT DUNVEGAN

The Beaver Indians of Dunvegan having met on this sixth day of July, in this present year 1899, Her Majesty's Commissioners, the Honourable James Hamilton Ross and James Andrew Joseph McKenna, Esquire, and having had explained to them the terms of the Treaty unto which the Chief and Headmen of the Indians of Lesser Slave Lake and adjacent country set their hands on the twenty-first day of June, in the year herein first above written, do join in the cession made by the said Treaty, and agree to adhere to the terms thereof in consideration of the undertakings made therein.

In witness whereof Her Majesty's said Commissioners and the Headman of the said Beaver Indians have hereunto set their hands at Dunvegan on this sixth day of July, in the year herein first above written.

Signed by the parties thereto,
in the presence of the
undersigned witnesses, after
the same had been read and
explained to the Indians by
the Reverend Joseph Le Treste
and Peter Gunn, Interpreters.

J.H. Ross,
J.A.J. McKenna, } Commissioners,

his
NATOOSE X Headman,
mark

A.E. Snyder, Insp., N.W.M.P.,
J. Le Treste,
Peter Gunn,
F.J. Fitzgerald.

SIGNING AT FORT CHIPEWYAN

The Chipewyan Indians of Athabasca River, Birch River, Peace River, Slave River and Gull River and the Cree Indians of Gull River and Deep Lake, having met at Fort Chipewyan on this thirteenth day of July, in this present year 1899, Her Majesty's Commissioners, the Honourable James Hamilton Ross and James Andrew Joseph McKenna, Esquire, and having had explained to them the terms of the Treaty unto which the Chief and Headmen of the Indians of Lesser Slave Lake and adjacent country set their hands on the twenty-first day of June, in the year herein first above written, do join in the cession made by the said Treaty, and agree to adhere to the terms thereof in consideration of the undertakings made therein.

In witness whereof Her Majesty's said Commissioners and the Chiefs and Headmen of the said Chipewyan and Cree Indians have hereunto set their hands at Fort Chipewyan on this thirteenth day of July, in the year herein first above written.

Signed by the parties thereto, in the presence of the undersigned witnesses after the same had been read and explained to the Indians by Peter Mercredi, Chipewyan Interpreter, and George Drever, Cree Interpreter.

A.E. SNYDER, Insp., N.W.M.P.,
P. MERCREDI,
GEO. DREVER,
L.M. LE DOUSSAL,
A. DE CHAMBOUR, O.M.I.,
H.B. ROUND,
GABRIEL BREYNAT, O.M.I.,
COLIN FRASER,
F.J. FITZGERALD,
B.F. COOPER,
H.W. McLAREN.

J.H. ROSS,
J.A.J. McKENNA, } *Treaty Commissioners,*

his
ALEX. X LAVIOLETTE, *Chipewyan*
mark   *Chief,*

his
JULIEN X RATFAT,
mark   } *Chipewyan*
his   *Headmen,*
SEPT. X HEEZELL,
mark

his
JUSTIN X MARTIN, *Cree Chief,*
mark

his
ANT. X TACCARROO
mark   } *Cree*
his   *Headmen*
THOMAS X GIBBOT
mark

SIGNING AT SMITH'S LANDING

The Chipewyan Indians of Slave River and the country thereabouts having met at Smith's Landing on this seventeenth day of July, in this present year 1899, Her Majesty's Commissioners, the Honourable James Hamilton Ross and James Andrew Joseph McKenna, Esquire, and having had explained to them the terms of the Treaty unto which the Chief and Headmen of the Indians of Lesser Slave Lake and adjacent country set their hands on the twenty-first day of June, in the year herein first above written, do join in the cession made by the said Treaty, and agree to adhere to the terms thereof in consideration of the undertakings made therein.

In witness whereof Her Majesty's said Commissioners and Chief and the Headmen of the said Chipewyan Indians have hereunto set their hands at Smith's Landing on this seventeenth day of July, in the year herein first above written.

Signed by the parties thereto,
  in the presence of the
  undersigned witnesses, after
  the same had been read and
  explained to the Indians by
  John Trindle, Interpreter.

A.E. SNYDER, Insp., N.W.M.P.,
H.B. ROUND,
J.H. REID,
JAS. HALY,
JOHN TRINDLE,
F.J. FITZGERALD,
WM. MCCLELLAND,
JOHN SUTHERLAND.

J.H. ROSS,   } Treaty
J.A.J. MCKENNA,   } Commissioners,
                his
PIERRE X SQUIRREL Chief,
              mark
                his
MICHAEL X MAMDRILLE, Headman,
              mark
                his
WILLIAM X KISCORRAY, Headman,
              mark

SIGNING AT FORT MCMURRAY

The Chipewyan and Cree Indians of Fort McMurray and the country thereabouts having met at Fort McMurray on this fourth day of August, in this present year 1899, Her Majesty's Commissioner, James Andrew Joseph McKenna, Esquire, and having had explained to them the terms of the Treaty unto which the Chief and Headmen of the Indians of Lesser Slave Lake and adjacent country set their hands on the twenty-first day of June, in the year herein first above written, do join in the cession made by the said Treaty, and agree to adhere to the terms thereof in consideration of the undertakings made therein.

In witness whereof Her Majesty's said Commissioner and the Headmen of the said Chipewyan and Cree Indians have hereunto set their hands at Fort McMurray, on this fourth day of August, in the year herein first above written.

Signed by the parties thereto, in the presence of the undersigned witnesses after the same had been read and explained to the Indians by Rev. Father Lacombe and T.M. Clarke, Interpreters.

J.A.J. McKenna, *Treaty Commissioner,*

Adam X Boucher, *Chipewyan Headman,*
his mark

Seapotakinum X Cree, *Cree Headman.*
his mark

A. Lacombe, O.M.I.,
Arthur J. Warwick,
T.M. Clarke,
J.W. Martin,
F.J. Fitzgerald,
M.J.H. Vernon.

SIGNING AT WAPISCOW LAKE

The Indians of Wapiscow and the country thereabouts having met at Wapiscow Lake on this fourteenth day of August, in this present year 1899, Her Majesty's Commissioner, the Honourable James Hamilton Ross, and having had explained to them the terms of the Treaty unto which the Chief and Headmen of the Indians of Lesser Slave Lake and adjacent country set their hands on the twenty-first day of June, in the year herein first above written, do join in the cession made by the said Treaty, and agree to adhere to the terms thereof in consideration of the undertakings made therein.

In witness whereof Her Majesty's said Commissioner and the Chief and the Headmen of the Indians have hereunto set their hands at Wabiscow [*sic*] Lake, on this fourteenth day of August, in the year herein first above written.

Signed by the parties thereto, in the presence of the undersigned witnesses after the same had been read and explained to the Indians by Alexander Kennedy.

A.E. SNYDER, INSP., N.W.M.P.,
CHARLES RILEY WEAVER,
J.B. HENRI GIROUX, O.M.I., P.M.,
MURDOCH JOHNSTON,
C. FALHER, O.M.I.,
ALEX. KENNEDY, Interpreter,
H.A. CONROY,
(Signature in Cree character),
JOHN McLEOD,
M.R. JOHNSTON.

J.H. ROSS, *Treaty Commissioner,*

JOSEPH X KAPUSEKONEW, *Chief,*

his / mark

JOSEPH X ANSEY, *Headman,*

his / mark

WAPOOSE X *Headman,*

his / mark

MICHAEL X ANSEY, *Headman,*

his / mark

LOUISA X BEAVER, *Headman.*

his / mark

ORDER IN COUNCIL

RATIFYING TREATY NO. 8

Canada, Statutes,
63 Victoria, A. 1900,
Sessional Paper No. 14

EXTRACT from a Report of the Committee of the Honourable the Privy Council, approved by His Excellency on the 20th February, 1900.

On a Memorandum dated 8th February, 1900, from the Superintendent General of Indian Affairs, submitting for Your Excellency's consideration the accompanying Treaty made by the Commissioners, the Honourable David Laird, James Andrew Joseph McKenna, Esquire, and the Honourable James Hamilton Ross, who were appointed to negotiate the same, with the Cree, Beaver, Chipewyan and other Indians inhabiting the territory,— as fully defined in the Treaty—lying within and adjacent to the Provisional District of Athabasca.

The Minister recommends that the Treaty referred to be approved, and that the duplicate thereof which is also submitted herewith, be kept of record in the Privy Council and the original returned to the Department of Indian Affairs.

The Committee submit the same for Your Excellency's approval.

JOHN J. McGEE,
Clerk of the Privy Council.

The Honourable
The Superintendent General of Indian Affairs.

REPORT OF COMMISSIONERS

FOR TREATY NO. 8

Canada, Statutes,
63 Victoria, A. 1900,
Sessional Paper No. 14

WINNIPEG, MANITOBA, 22nd September, 1899.

The Honourable
    CLIFFORD SIFTON,
        Superintendent General of Indian Affairs,
                Ottawa.

SIR.—We have the honour to transmit herewith the treaty which, under the Commission issued to us on the 5th day of April last, we have made with the Indians of the provisional district of Athabasca and parts of the country adjacent thereto, as described in the treaty and shown on the map attached.

The date fixed for meeting the Indians at Lesser Slave Lake was the 8th of June 1899. Owing, however, to unfavourable weather and lack of boatmen, we did not reach the point until the 19th. But one of the Commissioners—Mr. Ross—who went overland from Edmonton to the Lake, was fortunately present when the Indians first gathered. He was thus able to counteract the consequences of the delay and to expedite the work of the Commission by preliminary explanations of its objects.

We met the Indians on the 20th, and on the 21st the treaty was signed.

As the discussions at the different points followed on much the same lines, we shall confine ourselves to a general statement of their import. There was a marked absence of the old Indian style of oratory. Only among the Wood Crees were any formal speeches made, and these were brief. The Beaver Indians are taciturn. The Chipewyans confined themselves to asking questions and making brief arguments. They appeared to be more adept at cross-examination than at speech-making, and the Chief at Fort Chipewyan displayed considerable keenness of intellect and much practical sense in pressing the claims of his band. They all wanted as liberal, if not more liberal terms, than were granted to the Indians of the plains. Some expected to be fed by the Government after the making of treaty, and all asked for assistance in seasons of distress and urged that the old and indigent who were no longer able to hunt and trap and were consequently often in distress should be cared for by the Government. They requested that medicines be furnished. At Vermillion, Chipewyan and Smith's Landing, an earnest appeal was made for the services of a medical man. There was expressed at every point the fear that the making of the treaty would be followed by the curtailment of the hunting and fishing privileges, and many were impressed with the notion that the treaty would lead to taxation and enforced military service. They seemed desirous of securing educational advantages for their children, but stipulated that in the matter of schools there should be no interference with their religious beliefs.

We pointed out that the Government could not undertake to maintain Indians in idleness: that the same means of earning a livelihood would continue after the treaty as existed before it, and that the Indians would be expected to make use of them. We told them that the Government was always ready to give relief in cases of actual destitution, and that in seasons of distress they would without any special stipulation in the treaty receive such assistance as it was usual to give in order to prevent starvation among Indians in any part of Canada; and we stated that the attention of the Government would be called to the need of some special provision being made for assisting the old and indigent who were unable to work and dependent on charity for the means of sustaining life. We promised that supplies of medicines would be put in the charge of persons selected by the Government at different points, and would be distributed free to those of the Indians who might require them. We explained that it would be practically impossible for the Government to arrange for regular medical attendance upon Indians so widely scattered over such an extensive territory. We assured them, however, that the Government would always be ready to avail itself of any opportunity of affording medical service just as it provided that the physician attached to the Commission should give free attendance to all Indians whom he might find in need of treatment as he passed through the country.

Our chief difficulty was the apprehension that the hunting and fishing privileges were to be curtailed. The provision in the treaty under which ammunition and twine is to be furnished went far in the direction of quieting the fears of the Indians, for they admitted that it would be unreasonable to furnish the means of hunting and fishing if laws were to be enacted which would make hunting and fishing so restricted as to render it impossible to make a livelihood by such pursuits. But over and above the provision we had to solemnly assure them that only such laws as to hunting and fishing as were in the interested of the Indians and were found necessary in order to protect the fish and fur-bearing animals would be made, and they would be as free to hunt and fish after the treaty as they would be if they never entered into it.

We assured them that the treaty would not lead to any forced interference with their mode of life, that it did not open the way to the imposition of any tax, and that there was no fear of enforced military service. We showed them that, whether treaty was made or not, they were subject to the law, bound to obey it, and liable to punishment for any infringements of it. We pointed out that the law was designed for the protection of all, and must be respected by all the inhabitants of the country, irrespective of colour or origin; and that, in requiring them to live at peace with white men whom came into the country, and not to molest them in person or in property, it only required them to do what white men were required to do as to the Indians.

As to education, the Indians were assured that there was no need of any special stipulation, as it was the policy of the Government to provide in every part of the country, as far as circumstances would permit, for the education of Indian children, and that the law, which was as strong as a treaty, provided for non-interference with the religion of the Indians in schools maintained or assisted by the Government.

We should add that the chief of the Chipewyans of Fort Chipewyan asked that the Government should undertake to have a railway built into the country, as the cost of goods which the Indians require would be thereby cheapened and the prosperity of the country enhanced. He was told that the Commissioners had no authority to make any statement in the matter further than to say that his desire would be made known to the Government.

When we conferred, after the first meeting with the Indians at Lesser Slave Lake, we came to the conclusion that it would be best to make one treaty covering the whole of the territory ceded, and to take adhesions thereto from the Indians to be met at the other points rather than to make several separate treaties. The treaty was therefore so drawn as to provide three ways in which assistance is to be given to the Indians, in order to accord with the conditions of the country and to meet the requirements of the Indians in the different parts of the territory.

severalty?
· own land must be farmed.

In addition to the annuity, which we found it necessary to fix at the figures of Treaty Six, which covers adjacent territory, the treaty stipulates that assistance in the form of seed and implements and cattle will be given to those of the Indians who may take to farming, in the way of cattle and mowers to those who may devote themselves to cattle-raising, and that ammunition and twine will be given to those who continue to fish and hunt. The assistance in farming and ranching is only to be given when the Indians actually take to these pursuits, and it is not likely that for many years there will be a call for any considerable expenditure under these heads. The only Indians of the territory ceded who are likely to take to cattle-raising are those about Lesser Slave Lake and along the Peace River, where there is quite an extent of ranching country; and although there are stretches of cultivable land in those parts of the country, it is not probable that the Indians will, while present conditions obtain, engage in farming further than the raising of roots in a small way, as is now done to some extent. In the main the demand will be for ammunition and twine, as the great majority of the Indians will continue to hunt and fish for a livelihood. It does not appear likely that the conditions of the country on either side of the Athabasca and Slave Rivers or about Athabasca Lake will be so changed as to affect hunting or trapping, and it is safe to say that so long as the fur-bearing animals remain, the great bulk of Indians will continue to hunt and to trap.

The Indians are given the option of taking reserves or land in severalty. As the extent of the country treated for made it impossible to define reserves or holdings, and as the Indians were not prepared to make selections, we confined ourselves to an undertaking to have reserves and holdings set apart in the future, and the Indians were satisfied with the promise that this would be done when required. There is no immediate necessity for the general laying out of reserves or the allotting of land. It will be quite time enough to do this as advancing settlement makes necessary the surveying of the land. Indeed, the Indians were

rural planning

generally averse to being placed on reserves. It would have been impossible to have made a treaty if we had not assured them that there was no intention of confining them to reserves. We had to very clearly explain to them that the provision for reserves and allotments of land were made for their protection, and to secure to them in perpetuity a fair portion of the land ceded, in the event of settlement advancing.

After making the treaty at Lesser Slave Lake it was decided that, in order to offset the delay already referred to, it would be necessary for the Commission to divide. Mr. Ross and Mr. McKenna accordingly set out for Fort St. John on the 22nd of June. The date appointed for meeting the Indians there was the 21st. When the decision to divide was come to, a special messenger was despatched to the Fort with a message to the Indians explaining the delay, advising them that Commissioners were travelling to meet them, and requesting them to wait at the Fort. Unfortunately the Indians had dispersed and gone to their hunting ground before the messenger arrived and weeks before the date originally fixed for the meeting, and when the Commissioners got within some miles of St. John the messenger met them with a letter from the Hudson's Bay Company's officer there advising them that the Indians, after consuming all their provisions, set off on the 1st of June in four different bands and in as many different directions for the regular hunt: that there was not a man at St. John who knew the country and could carry word of the Commissioners' coming, and even it there were it would take three weeks or a month to get the Indians in. Of course there was nothing to do but return. It may be stated, however, that what happened was not altogether unforeseen. We had grave doubts of being able to get to St. John in time to meet the Indians, but as they were reported to be rather disturbed and ill-disposed on account of the actions of miners passing through their country, it was thought that it would be well to show them that the Commissioners were prepared to go into their country, and that they had put forth every possible effort to keep the engagement made by the Government.

The Commissioners on their return from St. John met the Beaver Indians of Dunvegan on the 21st day of June [*sic*] and secured their adhesion to the treaty.* They then proceeded to Fort Chipewyan and to Smith's Landing on the Slave River and secured the adhesion of the Cree and Chipewyan Indians at these points on the 13th and 17th days of July respectively.

In the meantime Mr. Laird met the Cree and Beaver Indians at Peace River Landing and Vermillion, and secured their adhesion on the 1st and 8th days of July respectively. He then proceeded to Fond du Lac on Lake Athabasca, and obtained the adhesion of the Chipewyan Indians there on the 25th and 27th days of July.

After treating with the Indians at Smith, Mr. Ross and Mr. McKenna found it necessary to separate in order to make sure of meeting the Indians at Wabiscow on the date fixed. Mr. McKenna accordingly went to Fort McMurray, where he secured the adhesion of the Chipewyan and Cree Indians on the 4th day of August, and Mr. Ross proceeded to Wabiscow, where he obtained the adhesion of the Cree Indians on the 14th day of August.

The Indians with whom we treated differ in many respects from the Indians of the organized territories. They indulge in neither paint nor feathers, and they never clothe themselves in blankets. Their dress is of the ordinary style and many of them were well clothed. In the summer they live in teepees, but many of them have log houses in which they live in the winter. The Cree language is the chief language of trade, and some of the Beavers and Chipewyans speak it in addition to their own tongues. All the Indians we met were with rare exceptions professing Christians, and showed evidences of the work which missionaries have carried on among them for many years. A few of them have had their children avail themselves of the

---

* The Commissioners actually signed the Treaty with the Beaver Indians at Dunvegan on the Sixth day of July.

advantages afforded by boarding schools established at different missions. None of the tribes appear to have any very definite organization. They are held together mainly by the language bond. The chiefs and headmen are simply the most efficient hunters and trappers. They are not law-makers and leaders in the sense that the chiefs and headmen of the plains and of old Canada were. The tribes have no very distinctive characteristics, and as far as we could learn traditions of any import. The Wood Crees are an off-shoot of the Crees of the South. The Beaver Indians bear some resemblance to the Indians west of the mountains. The Chipewyans are physically the superior tribe. The Beavers have apparently suffered most from scrofula and phthisis, and there are marks of these diseases more or less among all the tribes.

Although in manners and dress the Indians of the North are much further advanced in civilization than other Indians were when treaties were made with them, they stand as much in need of the protection afforded by the law to aborigines as do any other Indians of the country, and are as fit subjects for the paternal care of the Government.

It may be pointed out that hunting in the North differs from hunting as it was on the plains in that the Indians hunt in a wooded country and instead of moving in bands go individually or in family groups.

Our journey from point to point was so hurried that we are not in a position to give any description of the country ceded which would be of value. But we may say that about Lesser Slave Lake there are stretches of country which appear well suited for ranching and mixed farming: that on both sides of the Peace River there are extensive prairies and some well wooded country; that at Vermillion on the Peace two settlers have successfully carried on mixed farming on a pretty extensive scale for several years, and that the appearance of the cultivated fields of the Mission there in July showed that cereals and roots were as well advanced as in any portion of the organized territories. The country along the Athabasca River is well wooded and there are miles of tar-saturated banks. But as far as our restricted view of the Lake Athabasca and Slave River country enabled us to judge, its wealth, apart from possible mineral development, consists exclusively in its fisheries and furs.

In going from Peace River Crossing to St. John, the trail which is being constructed under the supervision of the Territorial Government from moneys provided by Parliament was passed over. It was found to be well located. The grading and bridge work is of a permanent character, and the road is sure to be an important factor in the development of the country.

We desire to express our high appreciation of the valuable and most willing service rendered by Inspector Snyder and the corps of police under him, and at the same time to testify to the efficient manner in which the members of our staff performed their several duties. The presence of a medical man was much appreciated by the Indians, and Dr. West, the physician to the Commission, was most assiduous in attending to the great number of Indians who sought his services. We would add that the Very Reverend Father Lacombe, who was attached to the Commission, zealously assisted us in treating with the Crees.

The actual number of Indians paid was:—

7	CHIEFS AT $32.00 ....$	224 00
23	HEADMEN AT $22.00	506 00
2,187	INDIANS AT $12.00	26,244 00
		$ 26,974 00

A detailed statement of the Indians treated with and of the money paid is appended.

We have the honour to be, sir,

Your obedient servants,

DAVID LAIRD,

J.H. ROSS,

J.A.J. McKENNA,

Indian Treaty Commissioners.

STATEMENT OF INDIANS PAID

ANNUITY AND GRATUITY

MONEYS IN TREATY NO. 8,

DURING 1899

STATEMENT of Indians paid Annuity and Gratuity Moneys in Treaty No. 8, during 1899.

	Chiefs	Headmen	Other Indians	Cash Paid each Band	Total Cash Paid
				$ cts.	$ cts.
LESSER SLAVE LAKE.					
Keenoostayo's Band (Crees)—					
Chief at $32	1	—	—	32 00	
Headmen at $22	—	4	—	88 00	
Other Indians at $12	—	—	241	2,892 00	
					3,012 00
Captain's Band (Crees)—					
Headmen	—	1	—	22 00	
Other Indians	—	—	22	264 00	
					286 00
PEACE RIVER LANDING.					
Duncan Tastawit's Band (Crees and Beavers)—					
Headmen	—	1	—	22 00	
Other Indians	—	—	46	552 00	
					574 00
VERMILLION.					
Ambroise Tete-Noire's Band (Beavers)—					
Chief	1	—	—	32 00	
Headmen	—	1	—	22 00	
Other Indians	—	—	148	1,776 00	
					1,830 00
Tall Cree Band (Crees)—					
Headmen	—	1	—	22 00	
Other Indians	—	—	33	396 00	
					418 00
RED RIVER POST, PEACE RIVER.					
Crees paid as part of Band—Cree Band at Vermillion—					
Indians	—	—	66	792 00	
					792 00

	Chiefs	Headmen	Other Indians	Cash Paid each Band	Total Cash Paid
				$ cts.	$ cts.
FORT CHIPEWYAN.					
Chipewyan Band—					
Chief	I	—	—	32 00	
Headmen	—	2	—	44 00	
Other Indians	—	—	407	4,884 00	
					4,960 00
Cree Band—					
Chief	I	—	—	32 00	
Headmen	—	2	—	44 00	
Other Indians	—	—	183	2,196 00	
					2,272 00
SMITH'S LANDING.					
Chipewyan Band—					
Chief	I	—	—	32 00	
Headmen	—	2	—	44 00	
Other Indians	—	—	280	3,360 00	
					3,436 00
FOND DU LAC.					
Chipewyan Band—					
Chief	I	—	—	32 00	
Headmen	—	2	—	44 00	
Other Indians	—	—	376	4,512 00	
					4,588 00
FORT McMURRAY.					
Cree and Chipewyan Bands—					
Headmen	—	2	—	44 00	
Other Indians	—	—	130	1,560 00	
					1,604 00
WABISCOW.					
Cree Band—					
Chief	I	—	—	32 00	
Headmen	—	4	—	88 00	
Other Indians	—	—	191	2,292 00	
					2,412 00
TOTAL	7	23	2187		26,974 00

STATEMENT of Indians paid Annuity and Gratuity, &c.—Concluded.

SUMMARY.

7	CHIEFS AT $32.00 ....$	224 00
23	HEADMEN AT $22.00	506 00
2,187	INDIANS AT $12.00	26,244 00
2,217	TOTAL ....$	26,974 00

Certified correct,

DAVID LAIRD,
J.H. ROSS
J.A.J. McKENNA
Indian Treaty Commissioners.

WINNIPEG, Man., September 22, 1899.

INDEX

Photograph page numbers refer to photographs on the opposite page and appear in italics. "ANN." refers to annotations in the frontmatter of the book. The terms "Treaty No. 8" and "Half-breed Scrip Commission" have not been indexed as these appear throughout the text, although the photographs have been indexed.

Department of Indian Affairs
1900.

MAP showing the Territory
ceded under treaty No.8,
and the Indian tribes therein.

Scale. 100 miles to an Inch.

TREATY No. 8.

MAP SHOWING

THE TERRITORY CEDED

UNDER TREATY NO. 8